Contents

ESSENTIAL
WASHINGTON   4–18

Introducing Washington   4–5
A Short Stay in Washington   6–7
Top 25   8–9
Shopping   10–11
Shopping by Theme   12
Washington by Night   13
Where to Eat   14
Where to Eat by Cuisine   15
Top Tips For…   16–18

WASHINGTON BY AREA 19–106
DOWNTOWN   20–32

Area Map   22–23
Sights   24–27
Walk   28
Shopping   29
Entertainment and Nightlife   30
Where to Eat   31–32

THE MALL   33–52

Area Map   34–35
Sights   36–50
Walk   51
Shopping   52
Where to Eat   52

CAPITOL HILL   53–68

Area Map   54–55
Sights   56–64
Walk   65
Shopping   66
Entertainment and Nightlife   67
Where to Eat   68

GEORGETOWN/
FOGGY BOTTOM   69–80

Area Map   70–71
Sights   73–75
Walk   76
Shopping   77–78
Entertainment
  and Nightlife   78–79
Where to Eat   80

NORTHWEST
WASHINGTON   81–94

Area Map   82–83
Sights   84–88
Walk   89
Shopping   90–91
Entertainment and Nightlife   92
Where to Eat   93–94

FARTHER AFIELD   95–106

Area Map   96–97
Sights   98–102
Excursions   103
Shopping   104
Entertainment and Nightlife   105
Where to Eat   106

WHERE TO STAY   107–112

Introduction   108
Budget Hotels   109
Mid-Range Hotels   110–111
Luxury Hotels   112

NEED TO KNOW   113–125

Planning Ahead   114–115
Getting There   116–117
Getting Around   118–119
Essential Facts   120–123
Timeline   124–125

D0106974

Introducing Washington

An equal mix of Southern gentility and Northern sophistication, America's capital is a microcosm of the United States, the melting pot's melting pot. Washington, D.C. is both quintessentially American and unique as an American city.

Washington is a city that was founded on politics because it was a compromise from the start. The site, close to George Washington's home at Mount Vernon, was chosen after a deal was brokered for the South to pay the North's Revolutionary War debts in exchange for having a southern capital. Virginia and Maryland donated land, and architect Pierre Charles L'Enfant (1754–1825) designed a city with a focal triangle formed by the Capitol, the president's house and a statue where the Washington Monument now sits.

L'Enfant also included plans for the Mall and diagonal boulevards crossing the grid of streets. L'Enfant's magnificent vision can be appreciated now, but for a long time the city was sparsely populated with unpaved avenues. Cattle grazed on the Mall and America's famous early leaders lived and worked in dank, dilapidated buildings.

This city is rich in things to see. Capitol Hill and the Mall, brimming with free museums, galleries and monuments, exhibit the range of America's wealth and artistry. The revitalized U Street and Columbia Heights reveal its cultural dynamism. Embassies have brought foreign delegations and friends, imbuing this relatively small city with pockets of cuisine and culture unavailable elsewhere in the U.S. And the arts scene is sophisticated, in part fueled by the droves of young professionals who move to the capital clamoring for powerful positions.

Although different types of businesses are moving to the city and helping to invigorate it, its core business remains government.

FACTS AND FIGURES

● The 230ft (70m) escalator at the Wheaton Metro station, in Montgomery County, is the longest in the western hemisphere.
● The Pentagon, at 6.6 millionsq ft (613,000sq m), is the world's third-largest building by floor area and has nearly 17.5 miles (28.2km) of corridors and 131 stairways.

TAXATION, REPRESENTATION?

Washington, D.C. license plates read "Taxation without Representation," a familiar refrain from the Revolutionary War. In this case the term alludes to the fact that the District lacks a voting representative in Congress. To add insult to injury, the Constitution also specifically gives Congress control over Washington's entire budget.

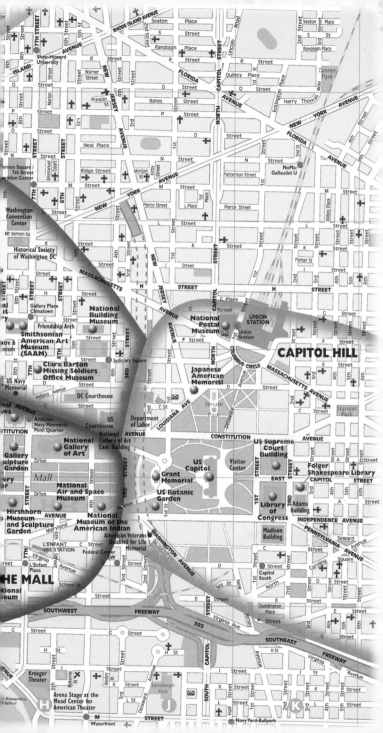

WASHINGTON D.C.

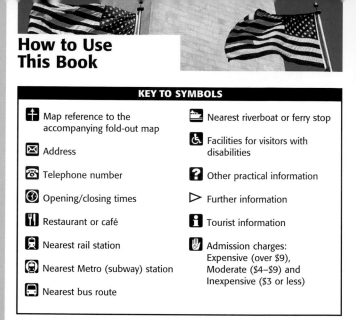

How to Use This Book

KEY TO SYMBOLS

✚ Map reference to the accompanying fold-out map

✉ Address

☎ Telephone number

🕒 Opening/closing times

🍴 Restaurant or café

🚆 Nearest rail station

Ⓜ Nearest Metro (subway) station

🚌 Nearest bus route

🚢 Nearest riverboat or ferry stop

♿ Facilities for visitors with disabilities

❓ Other practical information

▷ Further information

ℹ Tourist information

✋ Admission charges: Expensive (over $9), Moderate ($4–$9) and Inexpensive ($3 or less)

This guide is divided into four sections

● Essential Washington: An introduction to the city and tips on making the most of your stay.
● Washington by Area: We've broken the city into five areas, and recommended the best sights, shops, entertainment venues, nightlife and places to eat in each one. Suggested walks help you to explore on foot. Farther Afield takes you out of the city.
● Where to Stay: The best hotels, whether you're looking for luxury, budget or something in between.
● Need to Know: The info you need to make your trip run smoothly, including getting about by public transportation, weather tips, emergency phone numbers and useful websites.

Navigation In the Washington by Area chapter, we've given each area its own color, which is also used on the locator maps throughout the book and the map on the inside front cover.

Maps The fold-out map with this book is a comprehensive street plan of Washington. The grid on this fold-out map is the same as the grid on the locator maps within the book. We've given grid references within the book for each sight and listing.

D.C. ON FIRE

On August 24, 1814, as part of the on-going War of 1812, British soldiers entered Washington and began torching the town. They destroyed many buildings, including the Capitol and the White House, but not before dining on a feast hubristically prepared by First Lady Dolley Madison before she was forced to leave. Both buildings still retain scars from the incident.

SECOND SUBWAY

Members of Congress in a rush to vote need not break a sweat. In 1909, under-ground subway cars were installed to traverse the little more than 500ft (150m) between the Russell Senate Office Building and the Capitol. As subsequent office buildings were added, so were more train lines. These cars, most still open-top, continue to operate today.

A Short Stay in Washington

DAY 1

Morning Start your day at **Union Station** (▷ 66) and grab some coffee in the food court or a more substantial breakfast at the café in the main hall. Follow the flood of "Hill staffers" (▷ 123) as they head to work just before 9am. Most of them will stop at the Senate Office Buildings. You should too, if you have arranged a tour in advance. Otherwise head to the Capitol Visitor Center at the **U.S. Capitol** (▷ 60) and take a tour.

Lunch Head west out of the Capitol and onto the Mall. Either enjoy a meal of Native American delicacies at the **National Museum of the American Indian** (▷ 44) or lunch at the Cascade Café, with a view of the waterfall, at the **National Gallery of Art** (▷ 42).

Afternoon Stay on after lunch and take in an exhibition at either museum, neither of which will disappoint.

Mid-afternoon Walk west on the Mall past the Smithsonian museums to the **Washington Monument** (▷ 46). Take in the view south of the statue of Thomas Jefferson standing inside his memorial. Then look due north to see **The White House** (▷ 24) before walking toward it.

Dinner Walk up to Farragut North Metro station and take the train to Gallery Place–Chinatown Metro station before heading to lively **Jaleo** (▷ 32) for delicious Mediterranean tapas.

Evening After dinner, stop for a drink on the patio at **Dirty Habit** (▷ 30) before taking in a show at the **Shakespeare Theatre** (▷ 30) or **Woolly Mammoth** (▷ 30), depending on whether you like the Bard or avant garde.

DAY 2

Morning Start off the day at the **National Zoological Park** (▷ 84). Be sure to say hello to the pandas, the orangutans on the "O line" and the Komodo dragon, the first to be born outside of Indonesia.

Mid-morning Walk south on Connecticut Avenue and hop on the Metro to **Dupont Circle** (▷ 88). Or, if you stayed only a short time at the zoo, walk across the Calvert Street Bridge instead and take an immediate right down 18th Street through Adams Morgan.

Lunch If it's warm, try one of the outdoor cafés near Dupont Circle Metro's north entrance at Q Street or on 17th Street, or take a picnic to the Circle. There are also many good indoor options on Connecticut Avenue north and south of the Circle, and on P Street west of the Circle.

Afternoon Take the Metro to the Smithsonian station. Walk toward the **Washington Monument** (▷ 46) to 15th Street SW and take a left, heading toward the Tidal Basin, where you will find the **Martin Luther King, Jr., Roosevelt** and **Jefferson memorials** (▷ 39, 36).

Mid-afternoon Walk from the FDR Memorial north to the Reflecting Pool and the **Lincoln Memorial** (▷ 38), where Martin Luther King, Jr. delivered his "I Have a Dream" speech in 1963.

Dinner Enjoy the excellent food at the restaurants in the **Mandarin Oriental Hotel** (▷ 112), **Amity & Commerce** (▷ 52) for great views or the Empress Lounge if you're looking for something more casual.

Evening Catch a taxi to the **John F. Kennedy Center** (▷ 74), where, depending on the night, you can choose between ballet, opera, the symphony orchestra and world-class theater.

Top 25

► ► ►

Arlington National Cemetery ▷ 98–99 National heroes, like JFK, are buried here.

The White House ▷ 24–25 This icon is both the president's home and his office.

Washington National Cathedral ▷ 87 This Gothic cathedral is the sixth largest in the world and has held state funerals.

Washington Monument ▷ 46–47 The dynamic monolith is a striking memorial to America's first president.

Vietnam Veterans Memorial ▷ 48 A powerful memorial to the soldiers killed and missing in action in Vietnam.

U.S. Supreme Court Building ▷ 63 An austere building housing the highest court in the land.

U.S. Holocaust Memorial Museum ▷ 45 An unforgettable memorial to the millions exterminated by the Nazis in World War II.

FDR and Jefferson Memorials ▷ 36 Two beautiful memorials to two revered statesmen.

Frederick Douglass NHS ▷ 100 The former home of the anti-slavery abolitionist Frederick Douglass.

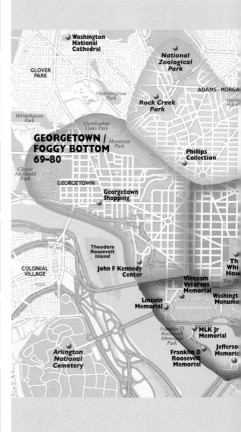

U.S. Capitol ▷ 60–61 Important debates of the day rage under this famous dome, which is also a showcase of Americana.

U.S. Botanic Garden ▷ 58–59 This elegant conservatory houses tropical and subtropical plants from around the world.

Rock Creek Park ▷ 86 This wooded gorge in the heart of Washington, D.C. is popular with hikers, bikers and joggers.

These pages are a quick guide to the Top 25, which are described in more detail later. Here they're listed alphabetically, and the tinted background shows which area they are in.

Georgetown Shopping ▷ **73** D.C.'s rich and powerful live and shop amid these tree-lined streets.

International Spy Museum ▷ **37** Learn about espionage through history at this fun museum.

John F. Kennedy Center ▷ **74** D.C.'s premier performing arts center hosting world-class performances.

Library of Congress ▷ **57** Jefferson's former collection is now a temple to the written word.

Lincoln Memorial ▷ **38** A somber monument to a complicated president.

Martin Luther King, Jr. Memorial ▷ **39** A fitting tribute to the American civil rights leader, set within parkland.

National Air and Space Museum ▷ **40** Soaring displays trace the progress of humankind reaching for the stars.

National Archives ▷ **41** America's scrapbook offers a first-hand peek at history.

National Gallery of Art ▷ **42** A treasure house of European and American art.

NMAAHC ▷ **43** Landmark museum dedicated to the African-American experience.

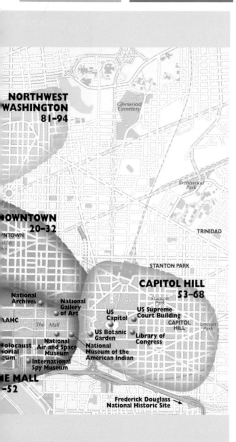

NORTHWEST WASHINGTON 81–94

Glenwood Cemetery

Brentwood Park

DOWNTOWN 20–32

TRINIDAD

STANTON PARK

CAPITOL HILL 53–68

National Archives

National Gallery of Art

US Capitol

US Supreme Court Building

Stanton Park

CAPITOL HILL

Lincoln Park

AAHC

The Mall

US Botanic Garden

Library of Congress

Holocaust Memorial Museum

National Air and Space Museum

National Museum of the American Indian

THE MALL 33–52

International Spy Museum

Frederick Douglass National Historic Site

Phillips Collection ▷ **85** Renowned collection of modern art in Phillips's Georgian Revival mansion.

National Zoological Park ▷ **84** The public's park is home to more than 2,000 animals from more than 400 species.

National Museum of the American Indian ▷ **44** Educational exhibits on America's first inhabitants.

◀ ◀ ◀

Shopping

A dive into Washington's shopping scene reveals that while District residents like having an assortment of fashionable stores at their disposal, it is intellectual pursuits like art, history and culture that may demand more of their money.

Shopping Areas

Shoppers who favor high-end designers and luxury brands like Caroline Herrera, Hugo Boss and Hermes will find them in Downtown's CityCenterDC complex, with Jimmy Choo, Tiffany and Neiman Marcus located in Friendship Heights and Chevy Chase. Lovers of vintage will discover treasures along the Adams Morgan strip, on U Street or 14th Street. Mainstream stores await in Downtown, Gallery Place, Georgetown and Pentagon City. Antiques and art hounds should head to Georgetown or Dupont Circle. Fashionable but hard-to-find styles for body and home can be found on Book Hill in Georgetown, along 14th Street and on U Street.

Book Worms

Washington is a book-lover's city. Every September the Library of Congress hosts the National Book Festival, which draws thousands to D.C. for talks and book signings by renowned authors and, naturally, the opportunity to purchase a title or two.

Independent stores, such as Kramerbooks and Politics & Prose, often include cafés and reading areas among their eclectic collections. Bridge Street Books in Georgetown, East City Bookshop on Capitol Hill and Upshur Street Books in Petworth are smaller but well-stocked

MARKET GEMS

Flea markets—open-air markets for secondhand items and antiques—occur every Sunday in Georgetown (1819 35th Street NW) and at Eastern Market (7th and C Streets SE). Dozens of vendors display art, jewelry, handicrafts, books, maps, china, linens and vintage clothes.

Clockwise from top left: Dupont Circle, Georgetown; stylish homeware and gifts;

options. Those hoping to spy an out-of-print or rare copy should search the aisles of used bookshops Carpe Librum (Downtown), Idle Time Books (Adams Morgan), Second Story Books (▷ 91), Capitol Hill Books (▷ 66) and Riverby Books (Capitol Hill).

Arts and Culture

Many arts museums, including the National Gallery of Art, Hirshhorn and Smithsonian American Art Museum, sell items ranging from exhibit catalogs to jewelry and high-quality prints. The National Building Museum carries a huge library of books on D.C. and the building arts. Fabrics, handicrafts, ceramics and precious stones from Asia and Africa are available at the Freer|Sackler galleries and the National Museum of African Art. The National Museum of the American Indian offers an expansive collection of Native American crafts.

U.S. History and Politics

No place outside Washington, D.C. offers the array of shopping options inspired by the multifaceted story of American democracy. Sites like the National Museum of American History, National Museum of African American History and Culture, U.S. Capitol Visitors Center, White House Historical Association and George Washington's Mount Vernon provide unparalleled opportunities to take home a piece of U.S. history. Souvenirs include a copy of the U.S. Constitution or Declaration of Independence, a biography of a U.S. president or Civil Rights leader, Federal-era candlesticks or fine china, a handmade quilt or needlepoint kit.

Chanel designer store; The Municipal Fish Market; Capitol Hill book store; city market and cafés

SOUVENIRS FOR KIDS

The multiple gift shops inside the National Museum of Natural History and National Air and Space Museum have large sections of items for children. Parents of budding politicians or young fans of the U.S. presidency will have a hard time extracting them from Honest Abe's Souvenirs and Washington Welcome Center, both in Downtown.

Shopping by Theme

Whether you're looking for a department store, a quirky boutique or something in between, you'll find it all in Washington. On this page shops are listed by theme. For a more detailed write-up, see the individual listings in Washington by Area.

Art and Antiques
Hemphill Fine Arts
(▷ 90)
Jean Pierre Antiques
(▷ 77)
National Gallery of Art
(▷ 52)
Torpedo Factory Art
Center (▷ 104)

Beauty and Skincare
Blue Mercury (▷ 77, 90)
Grooming Lounge (▷ 29)
Kiehl's (▷ 78)

Books
Bridge Street Books
(▷ 77)
Capitol Hill Books (▷ 66)
Kramerbooks (▷ 90)
Second Story Books
(▷ 91)

Clothing
Alden (▷ 29)
Anthropologie (▷ 77)
Betsy Fisher (▷ 90)
Coup de Foudre (▷ 29)
The Frye Company
(▷ 77)
hu's shoes (▷ 77)
J. Press (▷ 29)
Lilly Pulitzer (▷ 78)
Meeps (▷ 90)
Nordstrom Rack (▷ 29)
Proper Topper (▷ 91)
Raices (▷ 66)
Rizik's (▷ 91)
Secondi (▷ 91)
Village Art and Craft
(▷ 78)

Craft and Stationery
Fahrney's Pens (▷ 29)
Groovy DC Cards & Gifts
(▷ 66)
Jenni Bick Custom
Journals (▷ 90)
Just Paper and Tea
(▷ 78)

Food and Wine
A. Litteri (▷ 66)
Calvert Woodley Liquors
(▷ 90)
Eastern Market (▷ 66)
Glen's Garden Market
(▷ 90)
Hana Japanese Market
(▷ 90)

For Kids
Fairy Godmother (▷ 66)
National Air and Space
Museum (▷ 52)
National Museum of
the American Indian
(▷ 52)
National Museum of
Natural History (▷ 52)

Home Furnishings
A Mano (▷ 77)
American Holiday (▷ 77)
Anthropologie (▷ 77)
Good Wood (▷ 90)
Miss Pixie's (▷ 91)
Shop Made in DC
(▷ 91)
Tabletop (▷ 91)
Woven History and Silk
Road (▷ 66)

Jewelry
Tiny Jewel Box (▷ 91)

Malls
CityCenterDC (▷ 29)
Fashion Centre (▷ 104)
Friendship Heights
(▷ 104)
Gallery Place (▷ 29)
Potomac Mills Mall
(▷ 104)
Tanger Outlets (▷ 104)
Tysons Corner Center
(▷ 104)
Union Station (▷ 66)

Music
House of Musical
Traditions (▷ 104)
Smash Records (▷ 91)

Tobacconist
W. Curtis Draper (▷ 29)

Washington by Night

The mix of bustling restaurants, bars serving craft beer and handcrafted cocktails, arts venues and year-round sports events makes Washington a vibrant place at night. Hot spots around town are busy early and stay open late even on some week nights, especially in the warmer months when people seek outdoor and rooftop seating.

Going Out
Young professionals tend to head to areas like H Street and 14th Street, the popular places of the moment; Dupont Circle; Adams Morgan, which can get overcrowded with the 20-something crowd; Capitol Hill; and the especially lively area around the Clarendon Metro stop in Arlington, where many "Hill staffers" (▷ 123) live. The multitude of bars, cafés, live music venues, theaters and cinemas means there is something for everyone not only in downtown D.C., but also in its nearby neighborhoods and suburbs.

Monuments in the Moonlight
Perhaps the most inspiring, memorable evening experiences happen outdoors. The monuments and memorials, glorious in the sunlight, are entrancing in the moonlight. The Capitol looms on its hill over the Mall; the Lincoln Memorial stands guard at one end of Memorial Bridge, as does the Jefferson Memorial at the Tidal Basin; and the stark white Washington Monument is visible from most points in town. Tours by bus, Segway, bike, boat and foot bring these iconic sights to life. Visit the tourist information office for more on guided tours.

MOVIES ON THE LAWN
The Library of Congress (loc.gov) hosts an outdoor film festival on the north lawn of the library's Thomas Jefferson Building on Thursday nights from mid-July through mid-August, featuring iconic films from the library's National Film Registry. Bring a blanket and snacks and enjoy films like the *Wizard of Oz* and *E.T. The Extra-Terrestrial*.

Some of the many ways to spend an evening in Washington

Where to Eat

The Washington dining scene has come into its own in recent years as more and more residents have moved into the city and neighborhoods once deemed undesirable have become crowded with new cafés and restaurants. Fine dining, farm-to-table fare, small plates, upscale hamburgers, tasting menus—it's all here.

Top Chefs
Benefiting from lush expanses of nearby farmland and the seafood-rich Chesapeake Bay, the undeniable talent of chefs such as José Andrés (at Jaleo and Oyamel), Cathal Armstrong (at Kaliwa) and Fabio Trabocchi (at Fiola Mare) are taking cuisine to new levels. Their restaurants and others are no longer simply "good for D.C.," they're objectively a treat. Reservations are usually recommended for most establishments, unless an explicit "no reservations" policy is followed, which is an increasingly popular trend.

Street Food
A surefire way to sample the cuisine of the city's diverse population is to try the street food. On weekdays dozens of food trucks vie for prime parking spots and the choices are dazzling. Deluxe grilled cheese sandwiches, tacos, Maine lobster rolls and crab cakes pay tribute to the U.S., while other trucks offer tastes from Italy, Greece, Korea, Vietnam, Ethiopia, Mexico, El Salvador, Thailand—you crave it, you can find it. Look for food trucks outside the L'Enfant Plaza Metro station, at Franklin Park (McPherson Square Metro station), Farragut Park (Farragut West, Farragut North Metro stations), outside Metro Center and along the National Mall.

RESTAURANT WEEK

For a week each January and August, a host of D.C.'s restaurants, including some of its finest, offer three-course, fixed-price lunch and dinner menus for less than $50. Make reservations well in advance (ramw.org).

Expect stylish and delicious offerings in Washington's many restaurants

Where to Eat by Cuisine

There are plenty of places to eat to suit all tastes and budgets in Washington. On this page they are listed by cuisine. For a more detailed description of each venue, see Washington by Area.

American
Amity & Commerce
    (▷ 52)
Central (▷ 31)
Clyde's (▷ 31)
Corduroy (▷ 31)
Equinox (▷ 32)
Founding Farmers
    (▷ 32)
Good Stuff Eatery (▷ 68)
Komi (▷ 94)
The Majestic (▷ 106)
Rooster & Owl (▷ 94)
Rose's Luxury (▷ 68)
Sweet Home Café
    (▷ 52)
Ted's Bulletin (▷ 68)

Asian
Kaliwa (▷ 106)
Miss Saigon (▷ 80)
Pho 75 (▷ 106)
Sushiko (▷ 106)
Sushi Taro (▷ 94)
Teaism (▷ 94)
Thai Chef Street Food
    (▷ 94)
Toki Underground
    (▷ 106)

Burgers
Satellite (▷ 94)

Casual
Amsterdam Falafelshop
    (▷ 93)
Ben's Chili Bowl (▷ 93)
Busboys and Poets
    (▷ 93)

Ethiopian
Ethiopic (▷ 106)

European
Ambar (▷ 68)
Belga Café (▷ 68)
Leopold's Kafe and
    Konditorei (▷ 80)

French
Chez Billy Sud (▷ 80)
DBGB Kitchen & Bar
    (▷ 31)
Le Diplomate (▷ 93)
Green Pig Bistro (▷ 106)
Montmartre (▷ 68)

Indian
Indique (▷ 93)
Masala Art (▷ 52)
Rasika (▷ 32)

Italian
Carmine's (▷ 31)
Centrolina (▷ 31)

Latin
Guardado's (▷ 106)

Mediterranean
Fiola Mare (▷ 80)
Jaleo (▷ 32)
Kellari Taverna (▷ 32)
Lebanese Taverna
    (▷ 94)
Mezè (▷ 94)
Tail Up Goat (▷ 94)

Mexican
Oyamel (▷ 32)

**Picnics, Soups &
    Sandwiches**
Breadline (▷ 31)
Dog Tag Bakery (▷ 80)
Firehook (▷ 68)

Pizza
Pizzeria Paradiso (▷ 80)

Pub Food
Brixton (▷ 93)

Salads
Sweetgreen (▷ 80)

Seafood
Estuary (▷ 32)
Hank's Oyster Bar (▷ 93)
Market Lunch (▷ 68)

Steak
Bourbon Steak (▷ 80)
The Prime Rib (▷ 32)

Top Tips For...

These great suggestions will help you tailor your ideal visit to Washington, no matter how you choose to spend your time. Each sight or listing has a fuller write-up elsewhere in the book.

A BIRD'S-EYE VIEW

The observation deck of The Washington Monument (▷ 46–47) offers views sprawling 25 miles in every direction.

Sip cocktails at the POV roof terrace of the W Hotel (▷ 30) with a magnificent view of the Washington Monument.

Enjoy the 360-degree panorama over the Potomac and Foggy Bottom from the John F. Kennedy Center's terraces (▷ 74).

TRAIPSING AROUND TOWN IN FANCY SHOES

Enjoy a Cinderella moment at hu's shoes (▷ 77), an unparalleled selection of high-end women's footwear.

Or decide not to pay a fortune for a pair of shoes and instead go to Nordstrom Rack (▷ 29) for some real bargains.

DINING OUT OF THE BOX

Sample Austrian cuisine and mouthwatering pastries and cakes at Leopold's Kafe and Konditorei (▷ 80).

Dine on Ethiopian fare at Ethiopic (▷ 106), serving perfectly spiced meat dishes and a fantastic range of tasty vegetarian options.

PEOPLE-WATCHING

Claim a park bench in Dupont Circle (▷ 88) and watch D.C. natives scurrying to and from work or engaged in spirited conversation.

Drink in the history in the ornate lobby of the Willard Intercontinental (▷ 112), a short walk from the White House.

Observe the happy crowds and sleek motorboats gathering along the Potomac River at Sequoia (▷ 79).

Clockwise from top left: The Capitol; Rock Creek cyclists; Music at the Kennedy Center;

WATCHING WORLD-CLASS THEATER

Enjoy superbly acted and staged plays by Shakespeare and his peers at the Shakespeare Theatre (▷ 30).

Catch the world's best touring acts—from theater to music to dance—at the regal John F. Kennedy Center (▷ 74).

Go back in time and glimpse the avant garde at the home of the Woolly Mammoth Theatre Company (▷ 30).

BEING PAMPERED

Soak up the shaving lather in the plush Grooming Lounge (▷ 29).

Get the full treatment at the soothing spa in the Mandarin Oriental (▷ 112).

Enjoy the wellness-themed rooms, morning smoothies and yoga channel at Topaz Hotel (▷ 111), located in Dupont.

KEEPING MONEY IN YOUR POCKET

Visit the city's free locations, from the National Zoological Park (▷ 84), through all the Smithsonian museums to the National Gallery of Art (▷ 42).

Explore the more than 1,700 lush acres (687ha) of Rock Creek Park's recreational space (▷ 86).

Catch the daily free performance at the John F. Kennedy Center's Millennium Stage (▷ 74).

A GREAT SELECTION AT THE BAR

Sip one of the 30 plus by-the-glass wines at The Partisan (▷ 30).

Whet your whistle with the world's best beers at Birreria Paradiso (▷ 78).

Try a pint of Belgium's finest and tastiest at Belga Café (▷ 68).

Have a drink with the politicos at Hawk'n'Dove (▷ 67).

Enjoy a tune (and sing along if you're feeling brave) while supping a delicious cocktail at the Georgetown Piano Bar (▷ 79).

Willard Intercontinental Hotel; hu's shoes is one of many stores in Georgetown

ESSENTIAL WASHINGTON TOP TIPS FOR…

17

ESSENTIAL WASHINGTON TOP TIPS FOR...

KEEPING YOUR KIDS OCCUPIED

Let them create their own structures at the National Building Museum's "building zone" (▷ 26)—great fun.

Playfully interact with exhibits in Wonderplace at the National Museum of American History (▷ 50).

Help feed a tarantula at the National Museum of Natural History's Insect Zoo (▷ 50).

Let the Smithsonian Discovery Theater (▷ 49) dazzle with puppet shows, music and storytelling.

EATING WHERE LOCALS EAT

Take comfort in breakfast served all day at Ted's Bulletin (▷ 68).

Breathe in the aroma of fragrant teas and soothing soups at Teaism (▷ 94), a tea emporium like no other.

Browse the bookshelves or listen to a local activist before ordering your meal at Busboys and Poets (▷ 31, panel, 93).

GETTING OUTDOORS

Take time to appreciate the beautiful gardens at Dumbarton Oaks (▷ 75).

Wander among trees from almost every state at the National Arboretum (▷ 102)— a great escape from the city's hustle and bustle all year round but at its most memorable in the fall.

Enjoy the verdant Bishop's Garden (▷ 88) in the shadow of the National Cathedral (▷ 87).

SHOPPING WITH THE CHIC SET

Check out vintage home furnishings in the fun showroom that is Miss Pixie's (▷ 91) on 14th Street.

Window shop your favorite luxury brands before taking a gelato or coffee break at CityCenterDC (▷ 29).

Stop and pamper: Blue Mercury (▷ 77) is a high-end beauty shop from husband and wife Barry and Marla Beck—and this fashionable Georgetown store also offers spa services.

From top: National Museum of Natural History; afternoon tea at Teaism; innovative art brightens the city's streets

Washington by Area

Downtown 20–32

The Mall 33–52

Capitol Hill 53–68

Georgetown/Foggy Bottom 69–80

Northwest Washington 81–94

Farther Afield 95–106

Downtown

This area, stretching west from Chinatown to the White House, has boomed in the last few years and is the city's nerve center. The district is especially popular at night.

Top 25

The White House **24**

More to See **26**

Walk **28**

Shopping **29**

Entertainment and Nightlife **30**

Where to Eat **31**

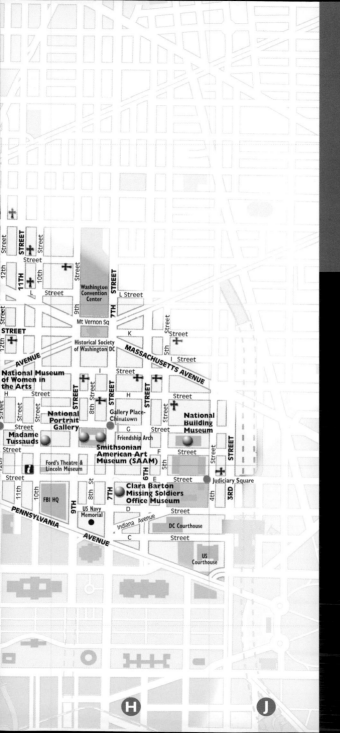

Street
STREET
12th
11TH
Street
10th
Street
L
9th Street

Washington
Convention
Center
7TH STREET
L Street

Mt Vernon Sq

12th Street
STREET
AVENUE
K

Historical Society
of Washington DC
5th Street
MASSACHUSETTS AVENUE
I Street

National Museum
of Women in
the Arts
H Street
8th Street
STREET
I Street
STREET
H Street

National
Portrait
Gallery
Gallery Place-
Chinatown

National
Building
Museum

Street
Madame
Tussauds
Street
G Street
5th Street

Smithsonian
American Art
Museum (SAAM)
Friendship Arch
Street

STREET
Ford's Theatre &
Lincoln Museum
F Street
Street
Judiciary Square

11th
10th
FBI HQ
9TH
8th St
7TH
US Navy
Memorial
Clara Barton
Missing Soldiers
Office Museum
E Street
4th
3RD STREET

PENNSYLVANIA
D Street
Indiana Avenue
DC Courthouse

AVENUE
C Street

US
Courthouse

H   J

The White House

THE BASICS

nps.gov/whho
whitehouse.gov
🚩 F5
✉ 1600 Pennsylvania
Avenue
☎ 202/456-7041
🕐 Tours by arrangement
only, Tue–Sat
💵 Free
♿ Excellent
Ⓜ McPherson Square,
Metro Center
❓ Write to a Member of
Congress three months in
advance to be accepted on
a free tour. Foreign visitors:
contact your embassy in
Washington. Some may
not be able to process
tour applications. For
historical exhibits: White
House Visitor Center, 1450
Pennsylvania Avenue
NW (🕐 Daily 7.30–4
Ⓜ Federal Triangle,
Metro Center)

In the city's oldest public building, virtually every desk, every sterling tea service, every silver platter, decanter, painting and floor has witnessed historic events of the American democracy.

The President's Palace When he became the second occupant in 1801 of what was then known as the President's Palace, Thomas Jefferson (1743–1826) thought the original design by James Hoban (c. 1762–1831) "big enough for two emperors, one Pope and the grand Lama." Since then the building has had several renovations. The first was after the British burned it in 1814, then another during the Truman Administration (1945–53) after a piano broke through the floor, and an engineer

Clockwise from left: 1600 Pennsylvania Avenue, the White House, first occupied as the President's Palace by John Adams in 1800; the east view looks toward the old Executive Building; the Washington Monument overlooking the White House

determined that the building was staying erect only out of "force of habit."

Works of art The White House holds an impressive display of decorative arts from the Sheraton, French, Queen Anne and Federal periods. There are carved marble mantels, Bohemian cut-glass chandeliers and Turkish Hereke carpets. The tour may vary depending on official functions, but usually includes the ceremonial East Room with Gilbert Stuart's 1797 *George Washington* portrait, the Vermeil Room containing 17th- and early 18th-century French and English gilded silver (vermeil), the small drawing room, and the State Dining Room where the *Abraham Lincoln* portrait by George P.A. Healy (1813–94) hangs.

HIGHLIGHTS

● *Abraham Lincoln*,
George P.A. Healy
● China Room
● French and English
gilded silver
● East Room
● *George Washington*,
Gilbert Stuart

More to See

CLARA BARTON MISSING SOLDIERS OFFICE MUSEUM

clarabartonmuseum.org

Barton's lodgings served as headquarters for her efforts to discover the whereabouts of missing Civil War soldiers.

➕ H6 ✉ 437 7th Street NW ☎ 202/824-0613 ⏰ Thu–Sat 11–6 (last entry at 5), Mon–Wed by appointment 🚇 Gallery Place–Chinatown, National Archives 💵 Expensive

DAR MUSEUM

dar.org/museum

The National Society of the Daughters of the American Revolution has been collecting pre-Civil War American artifacts for more than 100 years.

➕ F6 ✉ 1776 D Street NW ☎ 202/628-1776 ⏰ Mon–Fri 8.30–4, Sat 9–5 🚇 Farragut West, Farragut North 💵 Free

MADAME TUSSAUDS

madametussauds.com/washington

Take a tour through the glitterati of the world of politics, stage, screen and sport. Be interviewed in the Media Room and learn how the wax models are created.

➕ G5 ✉ 1001 F Street NW ☎ 202/942-7300 ⏰ Mon–Sat 10–6, Sun 10–5 (last admission 1 hour before closing) 🚇 Metro Center 💵 Expensive

NATIONAL BUILDING MUSEUM

nbm.org

The dramatic interior of this 19th-century building houses exhibits on D.C.'s cityscape, urban planning and architecture.

➕ H5 ✉ 401 F Street NW ☎ 202/272-2448 ⏰ Mon–Sat 10–5, Sun 11–5 🚇 Judiciary Square 💵 Expensive

NATIONAL GEOGRAPHIC MUSEUM

nationalgeographic.com

Best known for the *National Geographic Magazine*, the Society mounts exhibits about the world around us, and has displays of the work of its talented photographers.

➕ F4 ✉ 1145 17th Street NW ☎ 202/857-7700 ⏰ Daily 10–6 🚇 Farragut West, Farragut North 💵 Expensive

Madame Tussauds

NATIONAL MUSEUM OF WOMEN IN THE ARTS

nmwa.org

The only museum in the U.S. dedicated to the artwork of women, the collection includes around 5,000 objects by 1,000 artists from around the world, from the Renaissance to the present day

➕ G5 ✉ 1250 New York Avenue NW ☎ 202/783-5000 🕐 Mon–Sat 10–5, Sun 12–5 🚇 Metro Center 💷 Moderate

NATIONAL PORTRAIT GALLERY

npg.si.edu

This renovated neoclassical gallery has portraits of famous Americans crafted by other famous Americans using visual and performing arts and new media.

➕ H5 ✉ 8th and F streets NW ☎ 202/633-8300 🕐 Daily 11.30–7 🚇 Gallery Place–Chinatown 💷 Free

RENWICK GALLERY

americanart.si.edu/renwick

Housed in a lovely building, the Renwick is dedicated to American crafts and decorative arts, and hosts temporary exhibits.

➕ F5 ✉ 17th Street NW and Pennsylvania Avenue ☎ 202/633-7970 🕐 Daily 10–5.30 🚇 Farragut West, Farragut North 💷 Free

SMITHSONIAN AMERICAN ART MUSEUM (SAAM)

americanart.si.edu

Presidential portraits, folk art, video, photography and sculpture tell the story of America's rich artistic and cultural history from the colonial period to today.

➕ H5 ✉ 8th and F streets NW ☎ 202/633-7970 🕐 Daily 11.30–7 🚇 Gallery Place–Chinatown 💷 Free

WORLD BANK GROUP VISITOR CENTER

visitorcenter.worldbank.org

A fascinating showcase of the work the World Bank carries out across the globe to end poverty for the world's poorest people.

➕ F5 ✉ 1776 Pennsylvania NW ☎ 202/522 5000 🕐 Mon–Fri 10–5.30 🚇 Farragut West 💷 Free

National Portrait Gallery showcases 20th-century Americans

Presidential Route

Presidents parade down Pennsylvania Avenue as part of the inaugural celebrations. Reenact that procession with this walk.

DISTANCE: 2.25 miles (3.5km) **ALLOW:** 2 hours 45 minutes

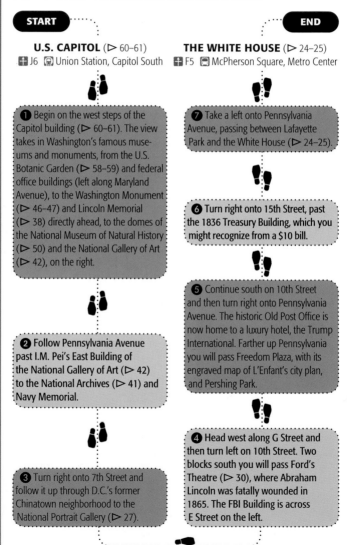

START

U.S. CAPITOL (▷ 60–61)
🚩 J6 🚇 Union Station, Capitol South

END

THE WHITE HOUSE (▷ 24–25)
🚩 F5 🚇 McPherson Square, Metro Center

❶ Begin on the west steps of the Capitol building (▷ 60–61). The view takes in Washington's famous museums and monuments, from the U.S. Botanic Garden (▷ 58–59) and federal office buildings (left along Maryland Avenue), to the Washington Monument (▷ 46–47) and Lincoln Memorial (▷ 38) directly ahead, to the domes of the National Museum of Natural History (▷ 50) and the National Gallery of Art (▷ 42), on the right.

❷ Follow Pennsylvania Avenue past I.M. Pei's East Building of the National Gallery of Art (▷ 42) to the National Archives (▷ 41) and Navy Memorial.

❸ Turn right onto 7th Street and follow it up through D.C.'s former Chinatown neighborhood to the National Portrait Gallery (▷ 27).

❼ Take a left onto Pennsylvania Avenue, passing between Lafayette Park and the White House (▷ 24–25).

❻ Turn right onto 15th Street, past the 1836 Treasury Building, which you might recognize from a $10 bill.

❺ Continue south on 10th Street and then turn right onto Pennsylvania Avenue. The historic Old Post Office is now home to a luxury hotel, the Trump International. Farther up Pennsylvania you will pass Freedom Plaza, with its engraved map of L'Enfant's city plan, and Pershing Park.

❹ Head west along G Street and then turn left on 10th Street. Two blocks south you will pass Ford's Theatre (▷ 30), where Abraham Lincoln was fatally wounded in 1865. The FBI Building is across E Street on the left.

DOWNTOWN WALK

Shopping

ALDEN

aldenshoe.com

Alden, originally of New England, sells good-quality men's shoes and boots in classic styles as well as a range of fine leather accessories.

➕ H5 ✉ 921 F Street NW ☎ 202/347-2308 🕐 Mon–Fri 10–6, Sat 11–5 🚇 Metro Center

CITYCENTERDC

citycenterdc.com/retail

You won't miss the five blocks of luxury shopping and high-end dining in the heart of Downtown. Dior and Hermes are here, as well as D.C. outposts of restaurants Momofuku and Del Frisco's.

➕ G/H5 ✉ 10th & H Street NW and New York Avenue NW ☎ 202/289-9000 🕐 Hours vary 🚇 Metro Center

COUP DE FOUDRE

coupdefoudrelingerie.com

"Love at First Sight" carries high-end European lingerie in its elegant boudoir and offers a fitting service.

➕ G6 ✉ Corner of 11th and E Street NW ☎ 202/393-0850 🕐 Mon–Sat 11–6 🚇 Metro Center

FAHRNEY'S PENS

fahrneyspens.com

This D.C. institution, started in 1929 by Earl Fahrney and still family owned, stocks traditional and cutting-edge pens and stationery as well as watches.

➕ G5 ✉ 1317 F Street NW ☎ 202/628-9525 🕐 Mon–Fri 9.30–6, Sat 10–5 🚇 Metro Center

GALLERY PLACE

galleryplace.com

Gallery Place complex has a movie theater, a bowling alley, restaurants, bars and popular retailers such as Urban Outfitters and Bed, Bath and Beyond.

➕ H5 ✉ 7th and H streets NW 🕐 Hours vary 🚇 Gallery Place–Chinatown

GROOMING LOUNGE

groominglounge.com

The Lounge pampers the modern male with grooming and shaving products, shaves and haircuts. You can even get a shoe shine while you're here.

➕ F4 ✉ 1745 L Street NW ☎ 202/466-8900 🕐 Mon–Fri 9.15–7, Sat 9–6, Sun 10–5.15 🚇 Farragut North, Farragut West

J. PRESS

jpressonline.com

This traditional clothier still strives to "dress men to the Ivy League standard." Head here for suits, blazers, ties and shirts in classic styles that were made to last.

➕ F4 ✉ 1801 L Street NW ☎ 202/857-0120 🕐 Mon–Fri 9–6.30, Sat 9.30–6 🚇 Farragut North, Farragut West

NORDSTROM RACK

nordstromrack.com

This popular discount clothing and shoe chain offers high-quality items from Nordstrom's department store at a fraction of the price. As well as women's and men's fashions, there's also a kids department and home furnishings.

➕ E4 ✉ 18th and L streets NW ☎ 202/627-3650 🕐 Mon–Fri 9–9, Sat 10–9, Sun 11–7 🚇 Farragut West

W. CURTIS DRAPER

wcurtisdraper.com

Founded in 1887, Draper has been offering a full array of cigars, pipes, pipe tobacco, snuffs and smoking accessories ever since.

➕ E4 ✉ 699 15th Street NW ☎ 202/638-2555 🕐 Mon–Fri 9.30–6.30, Sat 10–5 🚇 McPherson Square, Metro Center

Entertainment and Nightlife

DAR CONSTITUTION HALL
dar.org/constitution-hall
This historical 3,700-seat hall hosts music, stage shows and comedy acts. Past acts have included everyone from Billy Joel to Big Bird!
➕ F6 ✉ 18th and C streets NW ☎ 202/628-1776 🚇 Farragut West, then walk six blocks

DIRTY HABIT
dirtyhabitdc.com
The craft cocktails from this bar housed inside the Hotel Monaco can be sipped indoors or al fresco on a private patio. The bar and dining areas are all "film noir-inspired," making for a memorable evening out.
➕ H5 ✉ 555 8th Street NW ☎ 202/449-7095 🕐 Daily from 10.30am (closing times vary) 🚇 Gallery Place–Chinatown

FORD'S THEATRE
fordstheatre.org
Ford's, where Lincoln was shot, hosts plays and musicals, many for the family. Tours of the theater, a museum, exhibition on the aftermath of Lincoln's assassination, and entry into the house in which he died, are also available.
➕ G5 ✉ 511 10th Street NW ☎ 202/347-4833 🚇 Metro Center

THE HAMILTON
thehamiltondc.com
Classy venue for local blues, swing and R&B, and there's a frequent Gospel brunch. The Loft Bar of the restaurant also features late-night live music.
➕ G5 ✉ 600 14th Street NW ☎ 202/787-1000 🚇 Metro Center

THE PARTISAN
thepartisandc.com
Charcuterie from the adjoining butcher pairs perfectly with the drinks menu, featuring fun cocktails such as "Every time I eat vegetables" and over 20 interesting draft beers. Mouthwatering meals are also served throughout the day.
➕ H5 ✉ 709 D Street NW ☎ 202/524-5322 🕐 Daily from 11am (closing times vary) 🚇 Archives–Navy Memorial

POV ROOF TERRACE
povrooftop.com
Take in stunning views while indulging in superb cocktails and light bites in a fun and bright setting.
➕ G5 ✉ 515 15th Street NW ☎ 202/661-2437 🕐 Sun–Thu 12–12, Fri 11am–2am 🚇 McPherson Square

ROUND ROBIN BAR
washington.intercontinental.com
This circular bar maintains the same atmosphere it had in the 19th century when Senator Henry Clay introduced the bartender to the mint julep.
➕ G6 ✉ 1401 Pennsylvania Avenue NW ☎ 202/628-9100 🕐 Mon–Sat noon–1am, Sun 12–12 🚇 Metro Center

SHAKESPEARE THEATRE
shakespearetheatre.org
This theater presents high-quality productions of works by the Bard and other classics.
➕ H6 ✉ 450 7th Street NW (Lansburgh Theatre), 610 F Street NW (Sidney Harman Hall) ☎ 202/547-1122 🚇 Gallery Place–Chinatown

WOOLLY MAMMOTH THEATRE COMPANY
woollymammoth.net
New work from emerging playwrights is the staple of this often provocative resident troop.
➕ H6 ✉ 641 D Street NW ☎ 202/393-3939 🚇 Gallery Place–Chinatown

Where to Eat

BREADLINE ($)

breadline.com
This bakery-café makes everything on
the premises (and customers get a clear
view of the bakers and chefs at work),
including the warm rolls, salads, various
sandwiches and homemade soups.
⊞ F5 ✉ 1751 Pennsylvania Avenue NW
☎ 202/822-8900 ⏰ Mon–Fri 7–5.30
🚇 Farragut West

CARMINE'S ($–$$)

carminesnyc.com
Family-style Italian restaurant serving
huge portions of traditional Southern
Italian dishes.
⊞ H5 ✉ 425 7th Street NW ☎ 202/737
7770 ⏰ Sun–Thu 11.30–10, Fri–Sat 11.30–11
🚇 Archives–Navy Memorial

CENTRAL ($$$)

centralmichelrichard.com
This award-winning bistro serves
American cuisine with a French twist so
burgers sit happily alongside delicious
short rib bourguignon on the menu. It's
very popular so reserve ahead.

⊞ G6 ✉ 1001 Pennsylvania Avenue NW
☎ 202/626-0015 ⏰ Mon–Sat 11.30–2.30 and
5–10 🚇 Metro Center

CENTROLINA ($$$)

centrolinadc.com
Fans of chef Amy Brandwein praise her
regional Italian cooking on display here.
The open kitchen and modern design
make for a memorable and vibrant
lunch or evening meal out. There's also
a marketplace to buy delicious products.
⊞ G5 ✉ 974 Palmer Alley NW ☎ 202/898-
2426 ⏰ Mon–Sat 11.30–2.30, Sun–Thu 5–10,
Fri–Sat 5–10.30 (Market: Mon–Sun 11am–9pm)
🚇 Metro Center

CLYDE'S ($$)

clydes.com/gallery-place
There's something for everyone on the
vast American-fare menu in this soaring,
grand saloon and restaurant.
⊞ H5 ✉ 707 7th Street NW ☎ 202/349-
3700 ⏰ Mon–Thu 11am–2am, Fri–Sat
11am–3am, Sun 10am–2am 🚇 Gallery
Place–Chinatown

CORDUROY ($$–$$$)

corduroydc.com
You'll find Corduroy in a sleek, two-story
town house, with classy American fare
emphasizing seasonal ingredients.
⊞ H4 ✉ 1122 9th Street NW ☎ 202/589-
0699 ⏰ Mon–Sat 5.30–10.30 🚇 Mount
Vernon Square/Convention Center

DBGB KITCHEN & BAR ($$$)

dbgb.com
French haute cuisine meets casual
American fare in this city eatery. The
Baked Alaska is a must.
⊞ J5 ✉ 931 H Street NW ☎ 202/695-
7660 ⏰ Mon–Fri 11.30–3, Sun–Thu 5–10,
Fri–Sat 5–11, brunch Sat–Sun 11–3 🚇 Gallery
Place–Chinatown

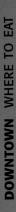

EQUINOX ($$$)

equinoxrestaurant.com

Chef Todd Gray builds beautiful, regional dishes, combining American cuisine and European influences. Still winning awards 30 years since it opened.

✚ F5 ✉ 818 Connecticut Avenue NW ☎ 202/331-8118 🕐 Mon–Fri 11.30–2, Mon–Sat 5.30–9.30, Sun 11–2 🚇 Farragut West

ESTUARY ($$$)

estuarydc.com

Focusing on seafood sourced from the Chesapeake Bay, there is always something for non-fish eaters on the menu. Imaginative fare from the Voltaggio brothers.

✚ G5 ✉ 950 New York Avenue NW ☎ 202/844 5895 🕐 Daily 11.30–2.30, Sun–Thu 5–10.30, Fri–Sat 5–11 🚇 Metro Center

FOUNDING FARMERS ($$)

wearefoundingfarmers.com

Describing itself as an "urban farmhouse," this restaurant is owned by a collective of farmers serving sustainable and seasonal food. Think hearty and soul-satisfying evening meals or weekend lunch.

✚ F5 ✉ 1924 Pennsylvania Avenue NW ☎ 202/822-8783 🕐 Mon 11am–10pm, Tue–Thu 11–11, Fri 11am–midnight, Sat 2–midnight, Sun 2–10pm 🚇 Farragut West, Foggy Bottom

JALEO ($$)

jaleo.com

A lively tapas restaurant, José Andrés' Jaleo serves up small plates that cater to any craving, whether it be for homemade chorizo or fried squid with aioli.

✚ H6 ✉ 480 7th Street NW ☎ 202/628-7949 🕐 Sun 10–10, Mon 11–10, Tue–Thu 11–11, Fri 11am–midnight, Sat 10am–midnight 🚇 Gallery Place–Chinatown

KELLARI TAVERNA ($$$)

kellaridc.com

Fresh whole fish is the signature offering at this convivial restaurant that pairs seafood with appetizers. Greek cuisine at its very best.

✚ F5 ✉ 1700 K Street NW ☎ 202/535-5274 🕐 Mon–Sat 11.30–10, Sun 11.30–9 🚇 Farragut West

OYAMEL ($$$)

oyamel.com

Another of chef and innovator José Andrés's ventures, serving Oaxacan cuisine and some of the best cocktails in town, all to be enjoyed with a colorful backdrop of a live, projected view of a Mexican market.

✚ H6 ✉ 401 7th Street NW ☎ 202/628-1005 🕐 Sun–Wed 11am–midnight, Thu–Sat 11am–2am 🚇 Archives

THE PRIME RIB ($$$)

theprimerib.com

The timeless elegance of a supper club is evoked by live piano music and a requirement for men to wear jackets at this meat-lovers paradise. Steakhouse classics such as seafood appetizers, rack of lamb and a selection of mouth-watering steaks draw many of the city's power brokers.

✚ E5 ✉ 2020 K Street NW ☎ 202/466-8811 🕐 Daily 5–10.30 🚇 Farragut West

RASIKA ($$–$$$)

rasikarestaurant.com

One of the city's top Indian restaurants, Rasika showcases *tawa* (griddle), *sigri* (open barbecue), tandoori and regional dishes, as well as small plates. Reservations are a must.

✚ H6 ✉ 633 D Street NW ☎ 202/637-1222 🕐 Mon–Fri 11.30–2.30, Mon–Thu 5.30–10.30, Fri–Sat 5–11 🚇 Archives–Navy Memorial

The Mall

Explore the grassy promenade from the Capitol to the Washington Monument.

Top 25

FDR and Jefferson Memorials **36**

International Spy Museum **37**

Lincoln Memorial **38**

Martin Luther King, Jr. Memorial **39**

National Air and Space Museum **40**

National Archives **41**

National Gallery of Art **42**

NMAAHC **43**

National Museum of the American Indian **44**

U.S. Holocaust Memorial Museum **45**

Washington Monument **46**

Vietnam Veterans Memorial **48**

More to See **49**

Walk **51**

Shopping **52**

Where to Eat **52**

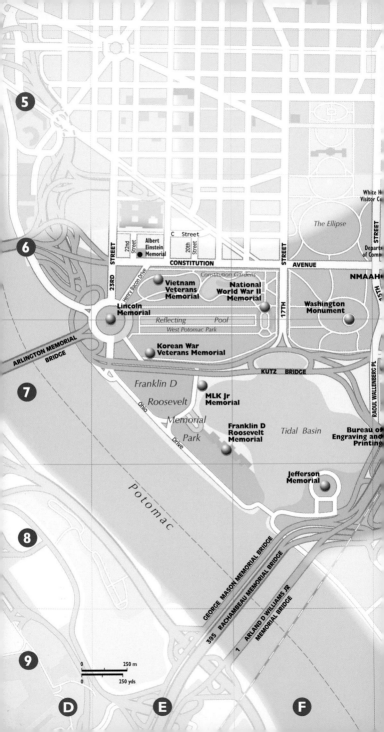

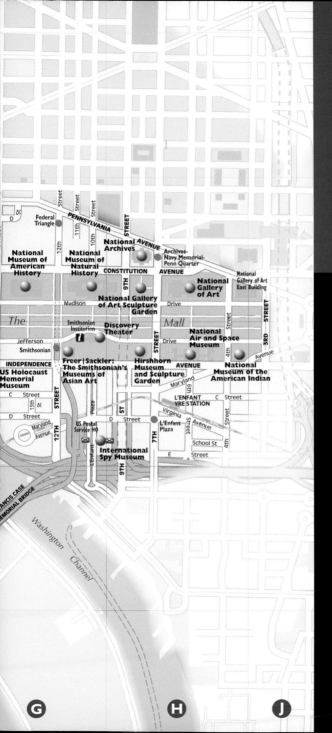

The Mall

FDR and Jefferson Memorials

TOP 25

Bronze statue of Thomas Jefferson (left); the Tidal Basin (right)

The Jefferson Memorial was dedicated by President Franklin Delano Roosevelt on the 200th anniversary of Jefferson's birth, April 13, 1943. Roosevelt's own memorial was created nearby and dedicated in 1997.

Classical The contributions of Thomas Jefferson, a brilliant statesman and America's third president, are commemorated in a white-marble, neoclassical memorial along Washington's Tidal Basin amid 3,800 Japanese cherry trees. The Memorial was modeled by architect John Russell Pope (1874–1937) on buildings that Jefferson had designed himself at his own home and the University of Virginia, which, in turn, gave a nod to the Pantheon in Rome. The open interior of the building has a 19ft (5.8m) bronze of Jefferson, encircled by excerpts of his speeches and writings inscribed into the walls. An inscription above Jefferson reads, "I have sworn upon the altar of God eternal hostility against every form of tyranny over the mind of man."

Sculpture Franklin Delano Roosevelt (1882–1945), America's president from the Great Depression through the end of World War II, is memorialized by a park on the west side of the Tidal Basin. The Memorial, cloaked in shady trees amid waterfalls and pools, is divided into four outdoor "rooms," each commemorating one of FDR's four terms in office. Nine sets of bronze sculptures, one of which is a depiction of FDR in a wheelchair, punctuate the park.

International Spy Museum

The International Spy Museum has the largest collection of espionage artifacts ever placed on public display. Plan to spend at least two hours.

Spies throughout history This is the place of dreams for anyone who's ever secretly wished they could cut it as a spy. Hundreds of historic artifacts, photographs, films and videos recall the most famous espionage events in history—from the Greek and Roman empires to the British Empire, both World Wars and, of course, the Cold War. Visitors receive a cover identity when they enter and learn about the tradecraft and tools of spying through the ages, watch films about real spies, and find out about the challenges facing today's spies. On the museum's fourth and fifth floors you can also visit the Briefing Center to come face-to-face with spymasters in Stealing Secrets, witness age-old techniques at Covert Action, and discover Spying that Shaped the World before heading to the Debriefing Center.

Undercover Mission You'll need to be a strategic thinker, have nerves of steel and a razor-sharp memory to take part in the museum's Undercover Mission, testing your spy skills as you travel around the permanent exhibits. Your performance is tracked and you'll receive a debrief upon conclusion of the mission by using the number on the reverse of your Undercover Mission badge. Check the website for further details.

THE BASICS

spymuseum.org

➕ G7

✉ 700 L'Enfant Plaza SW

☎ 202/393-7798

🕐 Times vary according to the date, so check online

✋ Expensive

♿ Excellent

🚇 L'Enfant Plaza

HIGHLIGHTS

● Interactive spy experiences
● An Uncertain World—how spy agencies protect us against threat

Lincoln Memorial

The Lincoln Memorial (left); sculpture of Lincoln (middle); Washington Monument (right)

THE BASICS

nps.gov/linc

✚ E6/7

✉ 2 Lincoln Memorial Circle between Constitution and Independence avenues (west end of the Mall)

☎ 202/426-6841

🕐 Daily 24 hours. Rangers available daily 9.30am–10pm

💵 Free

♿ Excellent

🚇 Foggy Bottom–GWU

HIGHLIGHTS

● Daniel Chester French's *Lincoln*
● Inscriptions of Lincoln's 1863 Gettysburg Address and Second Inaugural Address
● Reflecting Pool
● View at sunset

This powerful and majestic memorial honors the president who led the country through the Civil War and whose legacy gave rise to America's modern civil rights movement. The view from the steps at sunset is one of the city's most inspiring, with the Washington Monument reflected in the rectangular pool at its base.

Tribute Architect Henry Bacon (1866–1924) chose a Greek Doric style for this structure because he felt that a memorial to a man who had sacrificed so much to defend democracy should be modeled after the style found in the birthplace of democracy. Construction, during World War I, was not without difficulties. The marsh-like site required the builders to dig down almost 65ft (20m) to find a suitable foundation. Almost 38,000 tons of material was transported from as far away as Colorado.

History in stone Bacon's white marble temple to Lincoln contains a 19ft (6m) seated statue of the president by Daniel Chester French (1850–1931). The statue was so large that it had to be constructed inside the memorial. The chamber is flanked by two smaller rooms, which contain inscriptions of Lincoln's Gettysburg and second inaugural addresses and two beautiful murals. The area surrounding the Reflecting Pool, which stretches east from the foot of the monument, has hosted seminal events in America's history, most notably Martin Luther King, Jr.'s "I Have a Dream" speech.

Martin Luther King, Jr. Memorial

The statue of Martin Luther King, Jr. is the centerpiece of the memorial

Visitors to the Martin Luther King, Jr. Memorial take the same symbolic journey that the famous civil rights leader took—they pass through a boulder that has been split in two and named "Mountain of Despair" and emerge at the "Stone of Hope," a reference to his famous speech.

Years of planning It took more than two decades of planning and fundraising to realise this memorial to the famous American civil rights leader Martin Luther King, Jr. (1929–68), who followed Gandhi's philosophy of peaceful protest. The address of the white granite memorial, which was dedicated on October 16, 2011, is 1964 Independence Avenue SW, in commemoration of the year the Civil Rights Act became law.

A symbolic struggle The key message of the memorial is a line from King's "I Have a Dream" speech, which he delivered on the steps of the Lincoln Memorial in 1963: "Out of a mountain of despair, a stone of hope." Harry E. Johnson, president of the Memorial Project Foundation, said the 4-acre (1.5ha) site was "envisioned as a quiet and peaceful space, yet drawing from Dr. King's speeches and using his own rich language, the King Memorial will almost certainly change the heart of every person who visits…a public sanctuary where future generations of Americans, regardless of race, religion, gender, ethnicity or sexual orientation, can come to honor Dr. King."

THE BASICS

nps.gov/mlkm

🔲 F7

✉ 1964 Independence Avenue SW

☎ 202/426-6841

🕐 Daily 24 hours. Rangers available to answer questions daily 9.30am–10pm

💲 Free

♿ Excellent

Ⓜ Smithsonian, then a 15- to 20-min walk

❓ The memorial is located at the northwest corner of the Tidal Basin near the Franklin Delano Roosevelt Memorial

HIGHLIGHTS

● The Mountain of Despair
● The Stone of Hope
● Inscription wall with famous speech passages
● 29.5ft (9m) high stone relief of Dr. King

National Air and Space Museum

The Apollo lunar rover (left) and space rockets (right) are part of the collection

THE BASICS

airandspace.si.edu

➕ H7

✉ Jefferson Drive entrance (National Mall side)

☎ 202/633-2214

🕐 Daily 10–5.30

💲 Free

♿ Excellent

🍴 Wright Place Food Court

Ⓜ L'Enfant Plaza, Smithsonian

❓ Lockheed Martin IMAX, Udvar-Hazy IMAX: call for schedules. Tours daily

HIGHLIGHTS

● Wright brothers' *Flyer*
● Charles Lindbergh's *Spirit of St. Louis*
● Chuck Yeager's *Bell X-1 Glamorous Glennis*
● The Steven F. Udvar-Hazy Center
● John Glenn's *Friendship* and *Apollo 11*
● *Discovery* Space Shuttle
● Skylab Command Module
● Lunar exploration vehicles

One of the most visited museums on the Mall takes you on a pioneering journey from the first manned motorized flight to the most recent space exploration.

Flight pioneers The Smithsonian's bicentennial gift to the nation, this museum (in combination with its second location, the Steven F. Udvar-Hazy Center) receives almost nine million visitors a year in its monumental glass-and-granite galleries. The collection—begun as early as 1861—includes the Wright brothers' 1903 *Flyer*, Charles Lindbergh's *Spirit of St. Louis*, Chuck Yeager's *Bell X-1*, in which he broke the sound barrier, and *The Voyager*, the plane in which Dick Rutan and Jeana Yeager flew nonstop around the world in 1986.

Into space Visitors can touch a moon rock and see the *Apollo 11* and Skylab command modules, and the *Discovery* Space Shuttle. Aside from the Boeing Milestones of Flight Hall, there's exhibits on the space race between the United States and the Soviet Union, exploration of our solar system and the science of flight, among many others. Visitors who tire of the museum's colossal collection can take in an IMAX film, go for a test run in a flight simulator, or visit the Albert Einstein Planetarium and discover the universe. Despite its huge size, the building can only hold about 10 percent of the museum's collection. Most of the rest is housed in hangars at the Steven F. Udvar-Hazy Center near Dulles International Airport.

The National Archives (left); inspecting the Archives' historic documents (right)

Behind this building's colossal bronze doors, America's story comes alive through millions of items, including the founding documents, the rifle used to shoot John F. Kennedy (1917–63) and the Watergate tapes.

Charters of Freedom Under low light in the magnificent central rotunda lie 14 of America's founding documents, including the Constitution, the Declaration of Independence and the Bill of Rights. All have been encased in state-of-the-art, gold-plated, titanium frames filled with inert argon gas. Two 340lb (154kg) murals, *The Constitution* and *The Declaration of Independence*, accentuate the experience.

Archival splendor The Archives is most famous for the Charters of Freedom, but this building contains billions of other documents, maps and photographs, plus miles of film and videotapes, the most entertaining and instructional of which are on display in the Public Vaults. This child-friendly area showcases audio recordings of congressional debates on prohibition, video clips of former presidents cracking jokes and behind-the-scenes conversations between President Kennedy and his advisors during the Cuban Missile Crisis, among many other exhibits, all displayed in accessible multimedia presentations. The William G. McGowan Theater screens films about the Archives and the Charters of Freedom by day and documentaries at night.

THE BASICS

archives.gov
🚇 H6
✉ 700 Pennsylvania Avenue NW
☎ 1-866-272-6272 (toll free)
🕐 Daily 10–5.30
🎫 Free
♿ Excellent
Ⓜ Archives–Navy Memorial
❓ Guided tours Mon–Fri 9.45am (reservations required)

HIGHLIGHTS

● Charters of Freedom
● Murals by Barry Faulkner
● Changing exhibition gallery
● Hands-on activities in the Learning Center

THE MALL TOP 25

41

National Gallery of Art

TOP 25

The dome of the main atrium (left); National Gallery of Art East Building (right)

THE BASICS

nga.gov

H6

Between 3rd Street and 9th Street on Constitutional Avenue NW

202/737-4215

Mon–Sat 10–5, Sun 11–6

Free

Excellent

Cascade Café, Garden Café, Pavilion Café

Archives–Navy Memorial, Judiciary, Smithsonian

Tours daily

HIGHLIGHTS

- *Venus and Adonis*, Titian
- *The Alba Madonna*, Raphael
- *Laocoön*, El Greco
- *Daniel in the Lions' Den*, Peter Paul Rubens
- *Woman Holding a Balance*, Johannes Vermeer
- *A Girl with a Watering Can*, Auguste Renoir
- *Woman with a Parasol—Madame Monet and her Son*, Claude Monet
- *The Skater*, Gilbert Stuart

Housed in two distinctive buildings, the National Gallery contains one of the world's preeminent collections of paintings, drawings, sculptures and photographs ranging from the Middle Ages to the modern day.

West Building Designed by John Russell Pope in the classical style, this building was funded by a gift from Andrew Mellon, a former treasury secretary. Mellon also donated an impressive collection of art that has been expanded to fill the building's many galleries. Of particular interest are da Vinci's *Ginevra*, works by Vermeer and Monet, and a comprehensive collection of American art. The building is complemented by a large rotunda filled with flowers and the gentle sounds of a fountain, and by small garden courts in each wing of the building. The National Gallery frequently stages some of the nation's top temporary exhibitions (check online for details).

East Building This architectural masterpiece was created by I.M. Pei (b.1917), and opened in 1978. The galleries of the East Building are home to the modern art collection. Renovations marking the 75th anniversary of the gallery in 2016 added new gallery space and a stunning Roof Terrace that features several outdoor sculptures, including *Hahn/Cock* (a very large, very blue cockerel) by Katharina Fritsch on long-term loan. There are two new Tower Galleries, with works by Rothko and Calder.

NMAAHC exterior (left); a Cadillac from Chuck Berry's personal fleet (right)

At this landmark museum, on the Mall next to the Washington Monument, visitors can learn about the richness and diversity of African-American history, what it means to African-Amercan lives and how it helped shape the United States.

The new museum President George W. Bush signed the legislation establishing the National Museum of African-American History and Culture in 2003; the Smithsonian broke ground for the museum in February 2012. The 400,000sq ft (37,000sq m) building, with five levels above ground and four below, houses exhibition galleries, an education center, a theater, café and staff offices. A feature of the building is a series of openings—or lenses—in the exhibition spaces that frame views of the Washington Monument, the White House and other Smithsonian museums on the Mall. The aim of these views is to remind visitors that the museum presents a view of America through the lens of the African-American experience.

Exhibits The exhibitions focus on themes of history and community. Highlights include: a segregation-era railway car (*c.*1920), Nat Turner's Bible (*c.*1830s), Michael Jackson's fedora (*c.*1992), a slave cabin from Edisto Island, S.C. plantation (early 1800s), Harriet Tubman's hymnal (*c.*1876) and artworks by Charles Alston, Elizabeth Catlett and Henry O. Tanner.

THE BASICS

nmaahc.si.edu
🚩 G6
✉ 1400 Constitution Avenue NW
☎ 202/633-1000
🕐 Daily 10–5.30
♿ Free (passes required to enter). Check online for same-day passes and info on walk-up passes
♿ Excellent
🍴 Café
Ⓜ Smithsonian, Federal Triangle

HIGHLIGHTS

● Contemplative Court
● The Central Hall
● The reflecting pool
● Views from the museum
● The striking building

National Museum of the American Indian

TOP 25

The futuristic exterior (left); traditional shirt (middle); the rotunda display (right)

HIGHLIGHTS

● Limestone exterior and Grandfather Rocks
● Welcome Wall
● *Who We Are* film
● 20ft (6m) totem pole by Nathan Jackson
● Light-filled atrium
● Navajo weavings
● ImagiNATIONS Activity Center

The first national museum dedicated to Native Americans, this Smithsonian building pays homage to thousands of cultures with great cohesion.

Connection to nature The exterior, made out of Minnesota limestone, resembles a weatherworn rock mass, and the building sits on a serene 4.25-acre (1.7ha) plot with fountains and Grandfather Rocks (40 ancient rocks linking the Native American people to the environment). Inside, light is refracted from a prism in the ceiling into the museum's Potomac atrium, which often plays host to traditional ceremonies.

Break from tradition The museum breaks from the traditional anthropological treatment of Native Americans. "Our Universes" explores the spiritual relationship between humans and nature. "Return to a Native Place: Algonquian Peoples of the Chesapeake" informs visitors about the continued Native presence in the region. "Nation to Nation: Treaties between the United States and American Indian Nations" examines the history of U.S./American Indian diplomacy. The Red Power movement of the 1960s and 1970s is also highlighted. A large gallery space showcases the talents of Native American artists. The Lelawi Theater shows a spectacular film, *Who We Are,* to introduce the main themes of the museum. The Rasmuson Theater features storytelling, dance and music.

U.S. Holocaust Memorial Museum

This memorial to the millions of Jews and other targeted groups killed by the Nazis between 1933 and 1945 graphically portrays the personal stories and wider issues of persecution and human tragedy. The museum sets new standards for historical interpretation.

Disturbing "You cannot deal with the Holocaust as a reasonable thing," explained architect James Ingo Freed (1930–2005). To that end, he created a discordant building, intended to disturb the classical and sometimes placid facades elsewhere in Washington. Likewise, the central atrium, the Hall of Witness, disorients with twisted skylights, exposed load-bearing brick and architectural elements that don't join in conventional ways.

Nightmare Visitors are given identity cards that detail the life of a Holocaust victim as they enter a concise history of the rise of anti-Semitism in Europe, the Nazi party and the machinations of the Holocaust. The brilliant and shocking displays use high-tech audiovisuals. Some viewers are moved to tears. The Hall of Remembrance, a place for quiet reflection, is a welcome respite at the end of the experience. A special exhibit for children eight and over, "Daniel's Story," re-creates what life was like for a young boy trapped in the downward spiral of Nazi occupation. The Wexner Center, which holds temporary exhibitions, embodies the museum's continuing efforts to curb genocide.

THE BASICS

ushmm.org

🔲 G7

✉ 100 Wallenberg Place SW, south of Independence Avenue

☎ 202/488-0400

🕐 Daily 10–5.30. Closed Yom Kippur and Christmas Day

✋ Free

♿ Excellent

🍴 Vegetarian café

🚇 Smithsonian

❓ Timed, pre-booked tickets required between March and August. Check website for allocation release dates

HIGHLIGHTS

● Hall of Witness
● Hall of Remembrance
● For children (aged eight and over): "Daniel's Story"

Washington Monument

An icon of Washington life, this monolith is the world's tallest masonry structure and a memorable tribute to America's first president, George Washington (1732–99).

Rogues and cattle The Washington National Monument Society was founded in 1833 to solicit designs and funding for a memorial to America's first president. Construction began in 1848 but stopped in 1854 for over 20 years, in part because a rogue political party stole and destroyed a stone donated by the Pope. During this time, herds of Union cattle grazed on the grounds of the half-finished monument. A ring still betrays the slightly different marble that had to be used years later as construction began again amid the fervor

From far left: The Stars and Stripes flying in the breeze below the Washington Monument; the monument reflected in the Tidal Basin; the obelisk towering over the city of Washington

surrounding the centennial of the American Revolution. In 1884, 36 years after the cornerstone was placed, a 6.28lb (2.85kg) aluminum point—then one of the world's most expensive metals—was placed on top of the 555ft (169m) monument. At that time, this addition made it the tallest building in the world.

View The observation deck is 500ft (152m) above the ground. The views from the top cover most of Washington, as well as parts of Maryland and Virginia: look for the Tidal Basin, the Jefferson and Lincoln memorials, the White House, the U.S. Capitol, the Library of Congress and also the Smithsonian Institution. There are 193 commemorative stones donated by states, masonic lodges, church groups and foreign countries.

THE BASICS

nps.gov/wamo

✚ F6–F7

✉ The Mall at 15th Street NW

☎ 202/426-6841

🕓 Grounds: daily 24 hours. Interior daily 9–5 (reservation required)

♿ Excellent

Ⓜ Smithsonian

Vietnam Veterans Memorial

Glenna Goodacre sculpture (left); names of heroes on the black granite walls (right)

THE BASICS

nps.gov/vive

⊞ E6

✉ Near Constitution Avenue between 21st and 22nd streets NW, adjacent to the Lincoln Memorial

☎ 202/426-6841

🕐 Daily 24 hours

💲 Free

♿ Excellent

Ⓜ Foggy Bottom, then 15-min walk

❓ Rangers available to assist in locating names

HIGHLIGHTS

● Inscribed names
● Frederick Hart's sculptural group
● Glenna Goodacre's sculptural group
● Faces of visitors reflected in the polished stone

This black granite wall cut into the earth contains the names of service people killed during the Vietnam War. Despite a design process that was fraught with acrimony and misunderstanding (some suggested throwing the design out and starting again), the completed memorial has become one of the most revered sites in Washington.

Simple reminder Yale University student Maya Ying Lin (b.1959) was only 21 when she won the national design competition with a simple memorial—two triangular black granite walls, each 246ft (75m) long, set at a 125-degree angle and pointing toward the Washington Monument and Lincoln Memorial. The walls rise to 10ft (3m), seeming to overpower those who stand below. Names of soldiers who made the ultimate sacrifice for their country are listed chronologically. Between 1959 and 1975 more than 58,000 were killed or reported missing in action. In 1984 Frederick Hart's sculpture, *The Three Servicemen*, was dedicated at the south entrance, and in 1993 the *Vietnam Women's Memorial* by Glenna Goodacre was unveiled.

A place to reflect The polished surface reflects sky, trees, nearby monuments and the faces of visitors searching for the names of loved ones. Each day NPS Rangers collect mementoes left near soldiers' names and carefully place them in storage. Some are on display at the National Museum of American History (▷ 50).

More to See

BUREAU OF ENGRAVING AND PRINTING

moneyfactory.gov

A 40-minute tour, with introductory film, allows visitors to watch the powerful printing presses turn out millions of dollars every day.

➕ G7 ✉ 15th Street (temporary entrance) ☎ 866/874-2330 🕐 Visitor Center: Sep to mid-Mar Mon–Fri 8.30–2; mid-Mar to Aug 8.30–6 🚇 Smithsonian 🎫 Free but tickets required Mar–Aug. Booth on Raoul Wallenberg Place ❓ Renovations ongoing; check website for tour information

DISCOVERY THEATER

discoverytheater.org

Discovery Theater serves as a child's gateway to the exhibitions and collections contained in the Smithsonian museums on the National Mall and beyond.

➕ G7 ✉ 1100 Jefferson Drive SW ☎ 200/633-8700 🕐 Check online for schedule; there are no shows during Aug and Sep 🚇 Smithsonian 🎫 Inexpensive ❓ This is a popular stop for school groups so it can be busy

The Korean War Veterans Memorial

FREER|SACKLER: THE SMITHSONIAN'S MUSEUMS OF ASIAN ART

asia.si.edu

Connected by an underground passageway, these two museums represent the national museum of Asian art for the United States. In addition, the Freer Gallery contains an important collection of 19th-century American art.

➕ G7 ✉ 1050 Independence Avenue SW ☎ 202/633-1000 🕐 Daily 10–5.30 🚇 Smithsonian 🎫 Free

HIRSHHORN MUSEUM AND SCULPTURE GARDEN

hirshhorn.si.edu

This gallery showcases some first-rate art, including works by Henri Matisse, Man Ray and Andy Warhol. Temporary exhibitions display world-class contemporary artists.

➕ H7 ✉ 7th Street and Independence Avenue SW ☎ 202/633-4674 🕐 Daily 10–5.30. Garden 7.30am–dusk 🚇 L'Enfant Plaza 🎫 Free

KOREAN WAR VETERANS MEMORIAL

nps.gov/kowa

This memorial depicts 19 life-size figures marching through rugged terrain toward an American flag. The faces of 2,400 servicemen are etched into a wall nearby.

➕ E7 ✉ Adjacent to Lincoln Memorial ☎ 202/426-6841 🕐 Daily 24 hours 🚇 Foggy Bottom 🎫 Free

NATIONAL GALLERY OF ART SCULPTURE GARDEN

nga.gov

Many works by Bourgeois, Miró, Lichtenstein and other 20th-century

sculptors are on display in this garden, which is set around a fountain that transforms into an ice rink in winter.

➕ H6 ✉ Between Constitution Avenue and the Mall, 7th and 9th streets NW ☎ 202/737-4215 🕐 Mon–Sat 10–5, Sun 11–6 🍴 Pavilion Café 🚇 Archives–Navy Memorial 🎟 Free. Skating moderate

NATIONAL MUSEUM OF AMERICAN HISTORY

americanhistory.si.edu

From the original Star-Spangled Banner and Lincoln's top hat to Dizzy Gillespie's trumpet, exhibitions here cover many themes in U.S. history and culture.

➕ G6 ✉ Constitution Avenue and 14th Street NW ☎ 202/633-1000 🕐 Daily 10–5.30 🚇 Smithsonian, Federal Triangle 🎟 Free ❓ Tours

NATIONAL MUSEUM OF NATURAL HISTORY

mnh.si.edu

Beyond the African Elephant that presides over the entrance hall are permanent exhibits that explore ocean life, human origins and gems and minerals (including the Hope Diamond). Children will particularly enjoy the mummified cat, live butterfly pavilion (extra fee) and Sant Ocean Hall. Other galleries house changing displays.

➕ G6 ✉ Constitution Avenue and 10th Street NW ☎ 202/633-1000 🕐 Daily 10–5.30 🚇 Smithsonian, Federal Triangle 🎟 Free

NATIONAL WORLD WAR II MEMORIAL

nps.gov/nwwm

Formed around an open-air plaza and fountain, this memorial commemorates the sacrifices made by "The Greatest Generation" during World War II. Bronze bas-relief panels, granite columns, engraved quote and a wall of gold stars pay tribute to Americans who served in the military and on the home front.

➕ F6 ✉ The Mall at 17th Street SW ☎ 202/426-6841 🕐 Daily 24 hours 🚇 Smithsonian, then 10-min walk 🎟 Free

Display in the National Museum of American History

The National Museum of Natural History

Along the Mall

This walk along the grassy Mall will take you past D.C.'s most famous landmarks and give you a good look at the soul of the city.

DISTANCE: 3 miles (5km) **ALLOW:** 3 hours

START

U.S. CAPITOL (▷ 60–61)
➕ J6 🚇 Capitol South, Union Station

END

JEFFERSON MEMORIAL (▷ 36)
➕ F8 🚇 Smithsonian is a 15-min walk

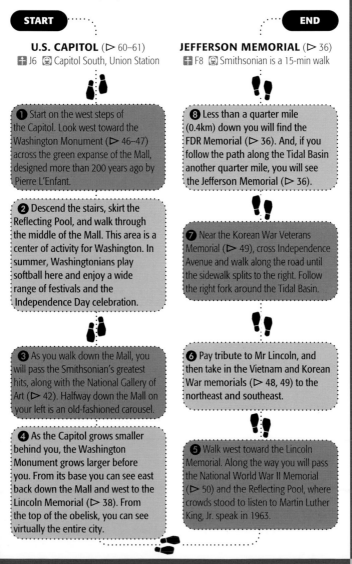

❶ Start on the west steps of the Capitol. Look west toward the Washington Monument (▷ 46–47) across the green expanse of the Mall, designed more than 200 years ago by Pierre L'Enfant.

❷ Descend the stairs, skirt the Reflecting Pool, and walk through the middle of the Mall. This area is a center of activity for Washington. In summer, Washingtonians play softball here and enjoy a wide range of festivals and the Independence Day celebration.

❸ As you walk down the Mall, you will pass the Smithsonian's greatest hits, along with the National Gallery of Art (▷ 42). Halfway down the Mall on your left is an old-fashioned carousel.

❹ As the Capitol grows smaller behind you, the Washington Monument grows larger before you. From its base you can see east back down the Mall and west to the Lincoln Memorial (▷ 38). From the top of the obelisk, you can see virtually the entire city.

❽ Less than a quarter mile (0.4km) down you will find the FDR Memorial (▷ 36). And, if you follow the path along the Tidal Basin another quarter mile, you will see the Jefferson Memorial (▷ 36).

❼ Near the Korean War Veterans Memorial (▷ 49), cross Independence Avenue and walk along the road until the sidewalk splits to the right. Follow the right fork around the Tidal Basin.

❻ Pay tribute to Mr Lincoln, and then take in the Vietnam and Korean War memorials (▷ 48, 49) to the northeast and southeast.

❺ Walk west toward the Lincoln Memorial. Along the way you will pass the National World War II Memorial (▷ 50) and the Reflecting Pool, where crowds stood to listen to Martin Luther King, Jr. speak in 1963.

THE MALL WALK

Shopping

NATIONAL AIR AND SPACE MUSEUM

airandspace.si.edu

A three-floor temple to aviation and souvenirs, this gift shop stocks toy rockets, model planes, kites and more.

🞦 H7 ✉ Jefferson Drive entrance (National Mall side) ☎ 202/633-2214 🕐 Daily 10–5.30 Ⓜ L'Enfant Plaza

NATIONAL GALLERY OF ART

nga.gov

In the West Building, this shop carries stationery, prints, scarves and jewelry, along with other items based on the current traveling exhibition.

🞦 H6 ✉ 6th Street and Constitution Avenue NW ☎ 202/737-4215 🕐 Mon–Sat 10–5, Sun 11–6 Ⓜ Archives–Navy Memorial

NATIONAL MUSEUM OF THE AMERICAN INDIAN

nmai.si.edu

This museum's gift shop sells high-grade textiles, jewelry and crafts made by Native American artisans.

🞦 H7 ✉ 4th Street and Independence Avenue SW ☎ 202/633-1000 🕐 Daily 10–5.30 Ⓜ L'Enfant Plaza

NATIONAL MUSEUM OF NATURAL HISTORY

mnh.si.edu

Five separate gift shops at this museum stock items ranging from dinosaur skeleton model kits to jewelry.

🞦 G6 ✉ Constitution Avenue and 10th Street NW ☎ 202/633-1000 🕐 Daily 10–5.30 Ⓜ Smithsonian

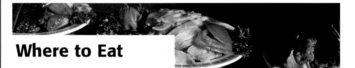

Where to Eat

AMITY & COMMERCE ($$$)

mandarinoriental.com/Washington

Curated signature dishes rotate daily to complement the delicious modern mainstays, which form the backbone of a menu that feels both bold and familiar, in this American bistro with an international flair.

🞦 H7 ✉ 1330 Maryland Avenue SW ☎ 202/5540-8588 🕐 Breakfast, lunch and dinner daily Ⓜ Smithsonian, then 10-min walk

MASALA ART ($$)

masalaartdc.com

Flavors of Northern India come to life in tandoori and *tawa* dishes here. A pretheater menu and weekend brunch attract many to this light-filled place.

🞦 H8 ✉ 1101 4th Street SW ☎ 202/554-1101 🕐 Dinner daily, lunch Mon–Fri, brunch Sat–Sun Ⓜ Waterfront

SWEET HOME CAFÉ ($)

nmaahc.si.edu/visit/sweet-home-cafe

In the NMAAHC, Sweet Home's menu highlights African-American cuisine using locally sourced ingredients. Reasonable prices make this a popular spot.

🞦 G6 ✉ 1400 Constitution Avenue NW ☎ 202/633-4751 🕐 Daily 10–5 Ⓜ Smithsonian, Federal Triangle

Capitol Hill

Dominated by federal buildings, Capitol Hill is home to the Capitol Building, Union Station, the Supreme Court and the Library of Congress. Neighborhoods of Victorian houses stretch east from these buildings.

Top 25

Library of Congress	**56**
U.S. Botanic Garden	**58**
U.S. Capitol	**60**
U.S. Supreme Court Building	**62**
More to See	**64**
Walk	**65**
Shopping	**66**
Entertainment and Nightlife	**67**
Where to Eat	**68**

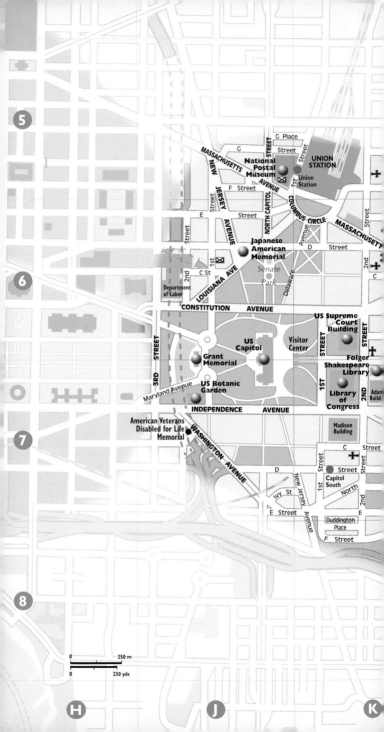

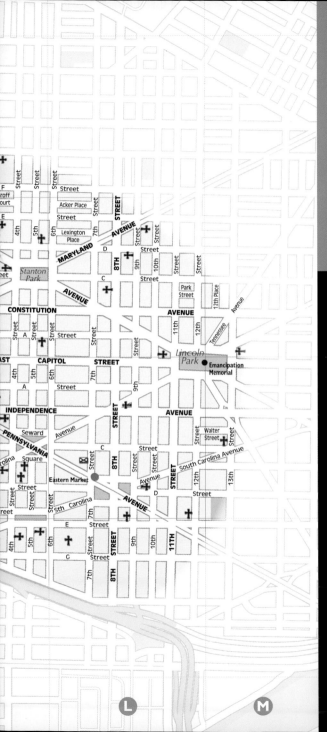

Capitol Hill

Library of Congress

One of the world's largest libraries, the de facto national library contains more than 168 million items, in 470 languages, on 838 miles (1,348km) of shelves. It welcomes scholars, the general public and, of course, Congress. The interiors of the main Jefferson Building are as ornate as their exterior would suggest.

A universal approach Congress appropriated funds for a library in 1800, but it was destroyed by the British when they burned the Capitol in 1814. Thomas Jefferson's personal library, one of the finest in the world, then became the nucleus of the new collection. Jefferson's approach to knowledge and book collection became the philosophy for the library itself, despite its intended purpose to be a resource for congresspeople and their staff. The library now files more than 15,000 new books a day, all copyrighted in the U.S.. The library has also collected random historical items including the contents of Lincoln's pockets on the evening he was shot, and original scores by Beethoven.

Room to read The Italian Renaissance Jefferson Building houses the library's Main Reading Room. A dozen figures representing the countries or empires that were pivotal in the creation of Western civilization look down from the apex of the 160ft (49m) dome. It is supported by columns topped by female figures representing aspects of civilized life, including religion, commerce, history and art.

THE BASICS

loc.gov

⊞ K7

✉ 1st Street and Independence Avenue SE

☎ 202/707-5000

🕐 Mon–Sat 8.30–4.30

✋ Free

♿ Excellent. Visitor Services (☎ 202/707-9779) has American Sign Language interpretation

🍽 Cafeteria, coffee shop, snack bars

Ⓜ Capitol South

❓ Tours begin at the Jefferson Building Mon–Sat 10.30, 11.30, 12.30, 1.30, 2.30, 3.30 (Sat no 12.30 and 3.30 tours). Resources are open to over-16s pursuing research

HIGHLIGHTS

● Torch of Learning on green copper dome
● Beaux Arts design
● Main Reading Room
● Sculpture inside and out
● View of the Capitol from the Madison Building cafeteria

CAPITOL HILL TOP 25

U.S. Botanic Garden

HIGHLIGHTS

- Seasonal displays
- Orchids and tropical plants
- Coffee, chocolate and banyan trees
- Bartholdi Fountain

TIPS

- Layered clothing is best as the temperatures in the glasshouses can be high.
- Temporary exhibits showcase different botanical themes.

A microcosm of climates in the U.S., the Botanic Garden lets you experience the desert of Arizona even when it's cold out. Blooms flower all year and December's poinsettia display is a real crowd pleaser.

Exotic glasshouse plants In 1838, Congress authorized Lieutenant Charles Wilkes—a surly captain said to be the inspiration for Melville's Captain Ahab—and his crew to circle the globe so that they might provide more accurate charts for the whaling industry. Wilkes returned in 1842 with a collection of exotic plant species, and Congress rekindled dormant plans for a botanical garden. The present conservatory, an attractive combination of iron-and-glass green-house and stone orangeries, was erected in 1933. With two outdoor gardens, the National

Clockwise from far left: The tranquil interior of the Conservatory Garden Court; lush tropical plants and trees in the massive glasshouse in the Botanic Gardens; the Rose Garden; Bartholdi Park Fountain and Conservatory

Garden and Bartholdi Park, the complex is home to more than 65,000 plants.

Flowers for all seasons The main entrance hall serves as a seasonal gallery displaying by turns tulips and hyacinths or chrysanthemums and Christmas poinsettias. The conservatory's 14 viewing areas feature plants grown for different uses and in different environments—from desert flora to the jungle, and from coffee and chocolate trees to plants that help fight cancer. Tucked in the gardens are four specimens—the Vessel Fern, the Ferocious Blue Cycad and two Sago Palms—that are believed to be directly related to those brought back on the Wilkes expedition. The fountain in the adjacent Bartholdi Park was sculpted by Frederic Bartholdi, designer of the Statue of Liberty.

THE BASICS

usbg.gov

🚩 J7

✉ 1st Street SW and Independence Avenue (100 Maryland Avenue SW)

☎ 202/225-8333

🕐 Conservatory daily 10–5. National Garden daily 7.30–5 (until 7pm in summer). Bartholdi Park dawn to dusk

🖐 Free

♿ Excellent

🚇 Federal Center

U.S. Capitol

HIGHLIGHTS

- Rotunda
- Frescoes by Constantino Brumidi
- Paintings by John Trumbull
- Visit to the House or Senate Chambers (not part of the Capitol tour—separate pass required)

TIP

- Enquire about Visitors Galleries passes at the House of Senate Appointments Desk in the Visitor Center.

The U.S. Capitol has stood on this hillside since the federal government came to the city in 1800. It is here that members of Congress go about their law-making work. A state-of-the-art Visitor Center explains this work and more.

Icon The 4,500-ton, cast-iron dome was an engineering feat when undertaken in 1851 by Capitol architect Thomas U. Walter and U.S. Army Captain Montgomery Meigs. It became a political symbol before it was even half finished: The Civil War broke out while it was under construction, and the Capitol housed the wounded. Many advised President Lincoln to halt work on the building, but he was adamant that progress continue as "a sign we intend the Union shall go on." The dome was completed in 1868.

Clockwise from far left: The famous dome of the U.S. Capitol; visitors inspecting the Rotunda; the Capitol is visible from nearly every part of the city, as it stands at the very heart of Washington; the stunning interior of the dome

Founding Fathers Visitors to the Capitol can tour the old Supreme Court Chamber, where famous cases have been decided; Statuary Hall, where the House of Representatives first met; the old Senate Chamber, where Webster, Clay and Calhoun famously sparred; and the ornate Brumidi Corridors (special tour Mon–Fri 11am and 2pm). But the crowning moment of the tour is the Rotunda, under the Capitol dome. Eight gigantic murals, four by George Washington's aide John Trumbull, depict scenes from the colonies and the revolutionary period. *The Apotheosis of Washington*, visible through the eye of the inner dome, depicts classical deities surrounding the first president. Constantino Brumidi (1805–80), who painted the fresco, was said to consort with prostitutes whose likenesses then appeared in the piece.

THE BASICS

visitthecapitol.gov

➕ J6–J7

✉ East Capitol and 1st Street

☎ 202/226-8000

🕐 Mon–Sat 8.30–4.30

💵 Free

♿ Excellent

🍴 Restaurant

🚇 Capitol South, Union Station, Federal Center

❓ Tours run Mon–Sat 8.50–3.20 and are free but require passes. U.S. citizens can ask their elected representatives; anyone can book online. A limited number of same-day passes are available daily at the information desks at the Visitor Center. Don't bring large bags such as backpacks, as they are prohibited

Clockwise from left: The
court's exterior; detail
of The Contemplation
of Justice

TOP 25

U.S. Supreme Court Building

The home of the highest judicial body in the United States, the Supreme Court, was not constructed here until 1935. Architect Cass Gilbert appears as a member of the sculpture group in the pediment over the entrance.

Judgments The court considers only cases that have far-reaching implications. The 1857 Dred Scott decision, which held that Congress had no authority to limit slavery, contributed to the onset of the Civil War. Rulings on abortion have frequently made the plaza in front of the building a focus of civil disobedience. *Brown v. Board of Education* required the integration of schools and bus travel across the land, and in 2015 the court ruled in favor of same-sex marriage nationwide. Justice Elena Kagan, appointed in 2010, is only the fourth woman to serve on the court in 231 years.

Law in action The steps up to the colonnaded entrance are flanked by two white-marble allegorical figures by James Earle Fraser, depicting *The Contemplation of Justice* and *The Authority of Law*. The magnificent bronze entrance doors lead into an entrance hall adorned with busts of all the former chief justices. When the court is in session you can join the "three-minute line" and glimpse the action from the Standing Gallery. A statue of John Marshall, Chief Justice from 1755 to 1835, dominates the street level, where a short film and exhibits describe the work of the court.

THE BASICS

supremecourt.gov

➕ K6

✉ 1st and East Capitol streets NE

☎ 202/479-3000

🕐 Mon–Fri 9–4.30

✋ Free

♿ Excellent

🍴 Cafeteria

Ⓜ Capitol South, Union Station

❓ Lectures on the half-hour when the court is not in session 9.30–3.30. A 24-min film about the building's history runs from 9.15–3.45

HIGHLIGHTS

● Bronze entrance doors
● Plaza sculpture
● Busts of chief justices
● Film and exhibits on court history
● The court in session

CAPITOL HILL TOP 25

63

More to See

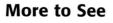

FOLGER SHAKESPEARE LIBRARY
folger.edu

The world's largest collection of Shakespeare's works is part of this library of 400,000-plus pieces from the European Renaissance. It's also home to the Folger Theater (▷ 67). Tour the library for an insight into Elizabethan England.

➕ K7 ✉ 201 E Capitol Street SE ☎ 202/544-4600 🕐 Mon–Sat 10–5, Sun 12–5. Library tours Mon–Sat 11, 1 & 3, Sun 12 & 3. Reading Room tours Sat at noon and Sun at 1. Garden closed through December 2019 🚇 Capitol South, Union Station 🎫 Free; performances expensive

GRANT MEMORIAL
aoc.gov

Cool and calm Ulysses S. Grant, Civil War general and former president, is honored atop his horse in this memorial, the largest equestrian statue in the U.S.

➕ J6–J7 ✉ 1st Street NW, at foot of Capitol Hill 🕐 Daily 24 hours 🚇 Federal Center SW 🎫 Free

JAPANESE AMERICAN MEMORIAL TO PATRIOTISM DURING WORLD WAR II
njamemorial.org

Although many Japanese Americans served in the U.S. military during World War II, others were regarded as potential spies and sent to internment camps. This poignant memorial represents the patriotism and hardships of both the veterans and those who endured captivity.

➕ J6 ✉ Louisiana Avenue & D Street NW 🕐 Daily 24 hours 🚇 Union Station

NATIONAL POSTAL MUSEUM
postalmuseum.si.edu

Rich displays ducument the history of the U.S. Postal Service with tributes to the Pony Express, airplanes, dog sleighs, 11 million stamps and interactive exhibits. This is a hidden gem of a museum and popular with families.

➕ J5 ✉ 2 Massachusetts Avenue NE, across from Union Station ☎ 202/633-5555 🕐 Daily 10–5.30 🚇 Union Station 🎫 Free

The Grant Memorial

Federal Route

Capitol Hill hums with activity during the working week. Take this walk to tap into the energy—and history—generated by Congress.

DISTANCE: 1.75 miles (3km) **ALLOW:** 2 hours

START

U.S. CAPITOL (▷ 60–61)
➕ J6 🚇 Capitol South, Union Station, Federal Center

END

EASTERN MARKET OR BARRACKS ROW (▷ 66) ➕ L7 🚇 Eastern Market

❶ Start at the U.S. Capitol (▷ 60–61) on Delaware Avenue. On the way you will pass the Russell Senate Office Building, where many Senators' offices and their staff are housed.

❼ From here you can enjoy some lively shopping at Eastern Market (▷ 66), north on 7th Street, or stop for food and drinks on bustling Barracks Row, south on 8th Street.

❷ If you don't have time to go inside the Capitol, take time to walk around it. Head west after you cross Constitution Avenue and follow the large circular path around the front of the Capitol.

❻ Depending on the time of day, you will see congressional staff grabbing a quick lunch or relaxing after a long day in the bars and restaurants that line the south side of Pennsylvania Avenue. Continue to the Eastern Market Metro stop.

❸ You will pass the Peace Monument before reaching the Grant Memorial (▷ 64) due west of the Capitol. Take the opportunity to climb the stairs for a view down the Mall toward the Washington Monument (▷ 46–47).

❺ The path ends at 1st Street SE and Independence Avenue. Taking Independence east you will pass the buildings of the Library of Congress (▷ 56–57) before turning right on Pennsylvania Avenue.

❹ Walk back down the stairs and continue south on the path around the Capitol. You will pass the Garfield Memorial and the U.S. Botanic Garden (▷ 58–59) before heading up the hill, with the House Office Buildings on your right.

Shopping

A. LITTERI

alitteri.com

In the heart of the wholesale market since 1932, this Italian shop stocks many types of olive oil and wines to go with any pasta dish you can dream up.

➕ L4 ✉ 517 Morse Street NE ☎ 202/544-0183 ⏱ Tue–Sat 9–8, Sun 11–6 Ⓜ NoMa–Gallaudet U, then 10-min walk

CAPITOL HILL BOOKS

capitolhillbooks-dc.com

This store is full of used books. Don't yodel too loudly—you might be crushed under an avalanche of books in the bathroom. Seriously, just don't.

➕ L7 ✉ 657 C Street SE ☎ 202/544-1621 ⏱ Mon–Fri 10–8, Sat 9–8, Sun 9–7 Ⓜ Eastern Market

EASTERN MARKET

easternmarket-dc.org

Here you'll find fresh produce under the canopy on weekends and fresh meats, fish, cheeses, baked goods and prepared foods six days a week. Saturday also brings a craft market, with a large selection of handmade jewelry.

➕ L7 ✉ 225 7th Street SE ☎ 202/698 5253 ⏱ Tue–Fri 7–7, Sat 7–6, Sun 9–5 Ⓜ Eastern Market

FAIRY GODMOTHER

A traditional and independent store catering to children of all ages, with a wide choice of books and classic toys.

➕ L7 ✉ 319 7th Street SE ☎ 202/547-5474 ⏱ Tue–Fri 11–6.30, Sat 9.30–5, Sun 11–5 Ⓜ Eastern Market

GROOVY DC CARDS & GIFTS

groovydc.com

This quirky card and gift shop sells lovely items such as journals, photo frames, candles, prints and local art.

➕ L7 ✉ 321 7th Street SE ☎ 202/544-6633 ⏱ Mon 12–6, Tue–Fri 11–7, Sat 10–5, Sun 11–5 Ⓜ Eastern Market

RAICES

raiceshandcrafts.com

Raices means "roots" in Spanish and this fair-trade and socially responsible store sells high-quality, handmade crafts imported from Ecuador, such as hats and scarves.

➕ L7 ✉ 225 7th Street SE ☎ 202/790-2728 ⏱ Sat–Sun 9–5 Ⓜ Eastern Market

UNION STATION

unionstationdc.com

The city's main transportation hub also doubles as a shopping mall where you can wander along marble-floored avenues. The stores are mostly national and international brands.

➕ K5 ✉ 50 Massachusetts Avenue NE ☎ 202/289-1908 ⏱ Mon–Sat 10–9, Sun 12–6 Ⓜ Union Station

WOVEN HISTORY AND SILK ROAD

wovenhistory.com

Selling Persian and tribal textiles, weavings and rugs, owner Mamet will charm and disarm you with detailed stories of his travels, and fascinating tales of how he has set up looms in refugee camps.

➕ L7 ✉ 315 7th Street SE ☎ 202/543-1705 ⏱ Tue–Sun 10–6 Ⓜ Eastern Market

MARKET MENU

For fresh produce and artisanal meats, check out Eastern Market (▷ above), Dupont Circle Market (1500 20th Street, NW; Sun 8.30–1.30), or Union Market (1309 5th Street NE; Mon–Wed, Sun 8–8, Thu–Sat 8am–9pm). All are great spots for picnic supplies.

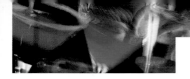

Entertainment and Nightlife

CAPITOL LOUNGE

capitolloungedc.com

The Cap Lounge, whose slogan is "No politics. No Miller Lite," is a sports bar at heart. Live games are shown on TV.

K7 ✉ 229 Pennsylvania Avenue SE
☎ 202/547-2098 🕐 Mon–Wed 4pm–2am, Thu–Fri 11am–2am, Sat 10am–3am, Sun 10am–2am 🚇 Capitol South

COOLIDGE AUDITORIUM

loc.gov

With its near-perfect acoustics and sightlines, this popular auditorium draws talented musicians from a broad range of genres. And the tickets are free.

K7 ✉ 101 Independence Avenue SE
☎ 202/707-5502 🚇 Capitol South

THE DUBLINER

dublinerdc.com

With all the friendliness you'd hope to find in one of its counterparts on the Emerald Isle, this Irish pub has been around for more than 45 years and remains a favorite with Senate staff. There is also daily live music.

J5 ✉ 4 F Street NW ☎ 202/737-3773
🕐 Sun–Thu 11am–1.30am, Fri–Sat 11am–2.30am 🚇 Union Station

FOLGER SHAKESPEARE LIBRARY

folger.edu

Don't expect to see a traditional enactment of the Bard's work in this re-creation of an Elizabethan theater, but delight in watching daring productions of Shakespeare's work.

K7 ✉ 201 East Capitol Street SE
☎ 202/544-4600 🚇 Capitol South

HAWK'N'DOVE

hawkndovebardc.com

This dark-wood-panel bar is the place to go to mingle with suited political folk and to feel close to the city's powerhouse. It is often frequented by lobbyists and interns.

K7 ✉ 329 Pennsylvania Avenue SE
☎ 202/547-0030 🕐 Mon–Thu 11am–midnight, Fri 11am–2am, Sat 10am–2am, Sun 10am–midnight 🚇 Capitol South

SONOMA WINE BAR

sonomadc.com

A soothing restaurant and bar with exposed brick walls and hardwood floors, offering a large selection of wine by the glass and a knowledgeable staff.

K7 ✉ 223 Pennsylvania Avenue SE
☎ 202/544-8088 🕐 Mon–Fri lunch, daily dinner 🚇 Capitol South

TUNE INN

Enjoy a cold beer overlooked by stuffed animal heads in this interesting booth-lined bar.

K7 ✉ 331 Pennsylvania Avenue SE
☎ 202/543-2725 🕐 Mon–Fri 8am–2am, Sat–Sun 8am–3.30am 🚇 Capitol South

SPECTATOR SPORTS

It's easy to catch a pro-sporting event in D.C. The Wizards and Mystics play basketball and the Capitals play ice hockey at the Capitol One Arena in Downtown. Baseball fans can head to Nationals Park, where the "Nats" take on the opposition. Buy tickets online or in person at stadium box offices.

MOVIES

Check the daily newspapers for mainstream movies. For art-house and foreign films, try Landmark's E Street Cinema (☎ 202/783-9494) or the Angelika Pop-Up at Union Market (550 Penn Street NE). The Library of Congress (☎ 202/707-5502) shows classic movies in its Mary Pickford Theater.

Where to Eat

PRICES

Prices are approximate, based on a 3-course meal for one person.

$$$ over $50
$$ $30–$50
$ under $30

AMBAR ($–$$)

ambarrestaurant.com

The first Balkan cuisine restaurant in DC, the menu includes a selection of "small plates," so have as many as you can.

L7 ✉ 523 8th Street SE ☎ 202/813 3039 🕐 Mon–Fri 11–2.30, Mon–Thu 4–10, Fri 4–11, Sat 4.30–11, Sun 4.30–10, brunch Sat–Sun 10–3.30 Ⓜ Eastern Market

BELGA CAFÉ ($–$$)

belgacafe.com

This smart Belgian restaurant serves the expected mussels and fries and fine Belgian beers as well as subtly flavored options. It's at its very best at brunch.

L8 ✉ 514 8th Street SE ☎ 202/544-0100 🕐 Mon–Fri 11–10, Sat–Sun 9am–9.30pm Ⓜ Eastern Market

FIREHOOK ($)

firehook.com

This popular bakery churns out tasty sandwiches on fresh-baked bread, along with tarts, pies, muffins and pastries.

K7 ✉ 215 Pennsylvania Avenue SE ☎ 202/544 7003 🕐 Mon–Fri 6.30am 7pm, Sat–Sun 7–5 Ⓜ Capitol South

GOOD STUFF EATERY ($)

goodstuffeatery.com

Don't mistake Good Stuff for a run-of-the-mill diner: everything is prepared with farm-fresh, high-quality ingredients.

K7 ✉ 303 Pennsylvania Avenue SE ☎ 202/543-8222 🕐 Daily 11–10 Ⓜ Capitol South

MARKET LUNCH ($)

marketlunchdc.com

This counter-service eatery in Eastern Market features crab cakes, fried fish and blueberry buckwheat pancakes.

L6 ✉ 225 7th Street SE ☎ 202/547-8444 🕐 Tue–Fri 7.30–2.30, Sat 8–3, Sun 9–3 Ⓜ Eastern Market

MONTMARTRE ($$)

montmartredc.com

A traditional but exceptional French bistro with an open-plan dining room and friendly environment.

L6 ✉ 327 7th Street SE ☎ 202/544-1244 🕐 Tue–Sun lunch, dinner, Sat–Sun brunch Ⓜ Eastern Market

ROSE'S LUXURY ($$–$$$)

rosesluxury.com

Chef Aaron Silverman has been praised for his "Southern comfort food threaded with globe-trotting ingredients." Only same-day reservations accepted.

L8 ✉ 717 8th Street SE ☎ 202/580-8889 🕐 Mon–Sat dinner Ⓜ Eastern Market

TED'S BULLETIN ($$)

tedsbulletin.com

The all-day breakfast is one of the draws at this fun, family-friendly establishment, serving American classics and adding a twist (think milk shakes with booze!).

L8 ✉ 505 8th Street SE ☎ 202/544-0337 🕐 Daily breakfast, lunch and dinner Ⓜ Eastern Market

UNION MARKET

Just beyond the northern boundary of Capitol Hill, this hub of all things locally made and artisanal offers Rappahannock oysters, tacos, local ice cream, empanadas and craft beer, as well as good-quality meats and fish.

Georgetown/ Foggy Bottom

D.C.'s oldest neighborhood started life as a tobacco port. Today well-heeled residents call this huge historic district home, with visitors attracted to Georgetown's outdoor shopping, especially when the sun shines.

Top 25

Georgetown Shopping **73**

John F. Kennedy Center **74**

More to See **75**

Walk **76**

Shopping **77**

Entertainment and Nightlife **78**

Where to Eat **80**

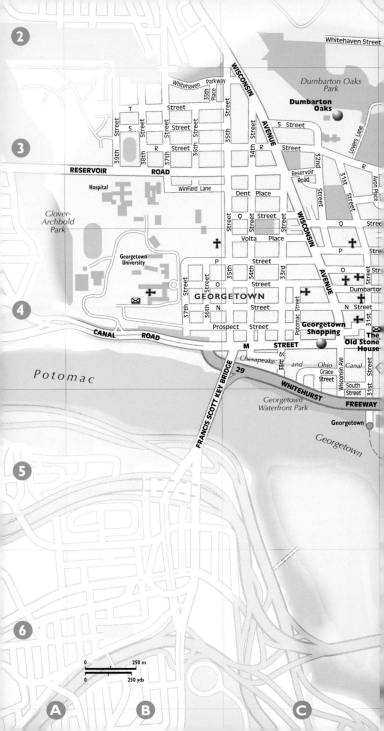

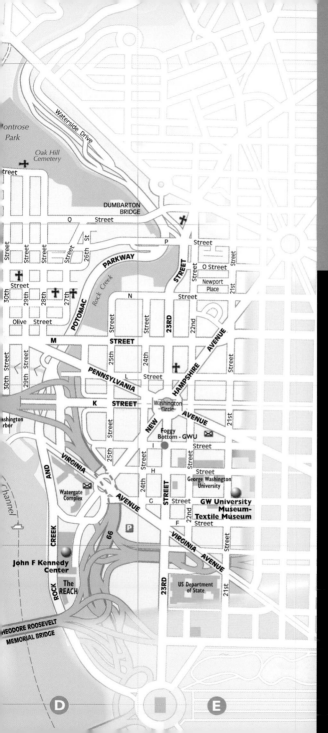

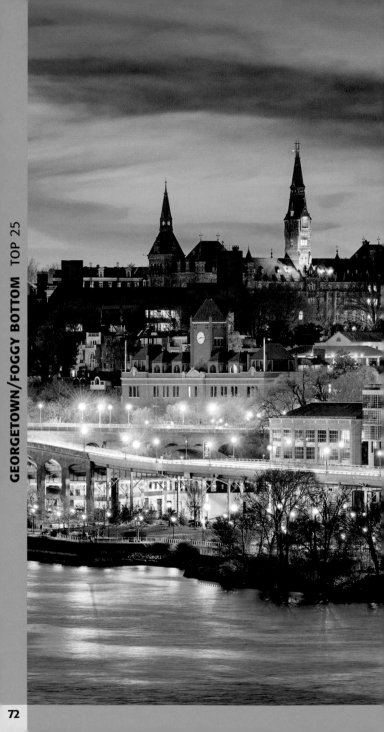

The legacy of residents like John and Jackie Kennedy and former *Washington Post* publisher Katharine Graham continues to give Georgetown an exclusive air, even though the village's heyday as the center of Washington's political and social life has passed. So it's no wonder that top-of-the-line retailers consider a Georgetown storefront highly desirable, with charming Federal-era buildings adding to the appeal.

Wisconsin and M Metro inaccessibility does not deter crowds from Georgetown's main intersection, full of chic shops that stretch north on Wisconsin Avenue and east on M Street. Warm months are particularly busy as tourists and locals flock to the stores such as Banana Republic, Urban Outfitters and Abercrombie & Fitch, as well as high-end beauty brands, among countless others.

Not just an outdoor mall You'll also find boutiques, antiques shops, home furnishings and bookstores. Dubbed "Georgetown's Design District," Cady's Alley, off 33rd Street just south of M Street, is lined with mid- to high-end home furnishing galleries. Georgetown's fine antiques shops can be found mainly on the eastern section of M Street before it crosses Rock Creek Parkway. Some of the better independent shops huddle farther up Wisconsin Avenue on Book Hill, just south of the Georgetown Library.

THE BASICS

✛ C4

✉ Mainly M Street NW between 30th Street and 34th Street and Wisconsin Avenue NW between South Street and R Street

♿ Limited

HIGHLIGHTS

● The shops at Georgetown
● A stroll along the C&O Canal towpath
● The view from the Georgetown Library
● Wandering among the Federalist mansions to the northeast of the intersection between Wisconsin Avenue and M Street

John F. Kennedy Center

A bust of Kennedy inside the Kennedy Center

TOP 25

THE BASICS

kennedy-center.org

📍 D6

✉ 2700 F Street NW

☎ 202/416-4600; 800/444-1324

🕐 Tours every 10 min Mon–Fri 10–5, Sat–Sun 10–1

♿ Free tours; performance ticket prices vary

🚻 Excellent

🍴 KC Café, Roof Terrace Restaurant ☎ 202/416-8555 for reservations

🕐 Café daily 11.30–8; restaurant dinner 5–8 before performances; brunch 11–2 most Sun

🚇 Foggy Bottom. Free shuttle bus every 15 min Mon–Fri 9.45am to midnight, Sat 10am–midnight, Sun 12–12, federal holidays 4pm–midnight

❓ Free Millennium Stage performance daily at 6pm

HIGHLIGHTS

● Hall of States
● View from the roof terrace
● Henri Matisse tapestries
● Well-stocked gift shop

With seven theaters, this national cultural center covers 8 acres (3ha) and is the jewel of the city's arts scene. The roof terrace provides a stunning 360-degree view of Washington and the Potomac.

The seat of the arts Opened in 1971, Edward Durell Stone's white-marble box overlooks the Potomac River next to the Watergate complex. The Center's inaugural performance featured the world premiere of a Requiem mass honoring President Kennedy, a work commissioned from composer and conductor Leonard Bernstein. As a living memorial to President Kennedy, the Center now hosts more than 3,000 performances a year by some of the world's most talented artists.

The interior The red carpet in the Hall of States, and the parallel Hall of Nations, leads to the Grand Foyer, where visitors are greeted by a 3,000lb (1,360kg) bronze bust of President Kennedy. The 630ft (192m) long hall blazes from the light of 16 Orrefors crystal chandeliers, donated by Sweden and reflected in 58ft-high (17.5m) mirrors, a gift from Belgium. If you take the tour, you'll see many other works of art and gifts from more than 60 countries. One end of the hall is devoted to the Millennium Stage, where free performances are given. The building also contains an opera house, a concert hall, two stage theaters, a jazz club and a theater lab. New in 2019, REACH is part of the center's expansion plans.

More to See

DUMBARTON OAKS

doaks.org

In 1944, the conference leading to the formation of the United Nations was held at this estate, also known for its formal garden, with an orangery, rose garden, wisteria and shaded terraces. This is a must-visit for anyone interested in gardens.

🔳 C3 ✉ 1703 32nd Street NW ☎ 202/339-6401 🕐 Museum Tue–Sun 11.30–5.30; garden 2–6 🚇 Dupont Circle, then bus D2 or D.C. Circulator bus 💲 Garden moderate; museum free

GEORGE WASHINGTON UNIVERSITY MUSEUM— THE TEXTILE MUSEUM

museum.gwu.edu

Three collections are united here: textile art representing six continents, the Albert A. Small Washingtoniana Collection of historic artifacts, and artworks from the university's collections.

🔳 E5 ✉ 701 21st Street NW ☎ 202/994-5200 🕐 Mon and Fri 11–5, Wed–Thu 11–7, Sat 10–5, Sun 1–5 🚇 Foggy Bottom, then 5-min walk 💲 Inexpensive

KREEGER MUSEUM

kreegermuseum.org

Built by David and Carmen Kreeger, this Philip Johnson mansion now houses art, predominantly the work of male masters of the last two centuries.

🔳 Off map at A3 ✉ 2401 Foxhall Road NW ☎ 202/338-3552 🕐 Tue–Sat 10–4 (tours Tue–Fri 10.30, 1.30; Sat 10.30, 12, 2) 🚇 Tenleytown, then taxi 💲 Expensive

THE OLD STONE HOUSE

nps.gov/olst

The oldest house in the city, dating from 1765, commemorates the daily lives of the early residents of Georgetown and is a rare example of pre-Revolutionary architecture. Among the artifacts is a clock built by one of the former owners of the house.

🔳 D4 ✉ 3051 M Street NW ☎ 202/426-6851 🕐 Daily 11–7 🚇 Foggy Bottom, then 10-min walk 💲 Free

A demonstration at the Textile Museum

The Fountain Terrace, Dumbarton Oaks

Waterfront Walk

See one of Washington's oldest and most stately neighborhoods from a variety of angles and perspectives.

DISTANCE: 1.5 miles (2.5km) **ALLOW:** 2 hours

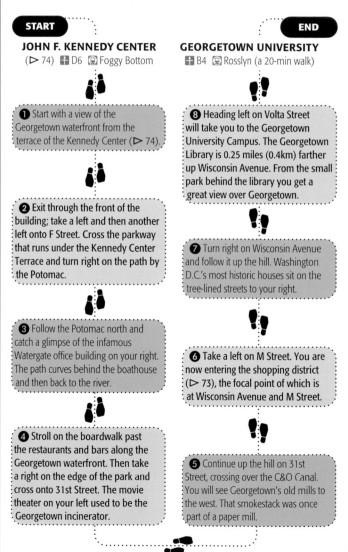

START

JOHN F. KENNEDY CENTER
(▷ 74) 🔢 D6 🚇 Foggy Bottom

1 Start with a view of the Georgetown waterfront from the terrace of the Kennedy Center (▷ 74).

2 Exit through the front of the building; take a left and then another left onto F Street. Cross the parkway that runs under the Kennedy Center Terrace and turn right on the path by the Potomac.

3 Follow the Potomac north and catch a glimpse of the infamous Watergate office building on your right. The path curves behind the boathouse and then back to the river.

4 Stroll on the boardwalk past the restaurants and bars along the Georgetown waterfront. Then take a right on the edge of the park and cross onto 31st Street. The movie theater on your left used to be the Georgetown incinerator.

END

GEORGETOWN UNIVERSITY
🔢 B4 🚇 Rosslyn (a 20-min walk)

8 Heading left on Volta Street will take you to the Georgetown University Campus. The Georgetown Library is 0.25 miles (0.4km) farther up Wisconsin Avenue. From the small park behind the library you get a great view over Georgetown.

7 Turn right on Wisconsin Avenue and follow it up the hill. Washington D.C.'s most historic houses sit on the tree-lined streets to your right.

6 Take a left on M Street. You are now entering the shopping district (▷ 73), the focal point of which is at Wisconsin Avenue and M Street.

5 Continue up the hill on 31st Street, crossing over the C&O Canal. You will see Georgetown's old mills to the west. That smokestack was once part of a paper mill.

Shopping

A MANO

amano.bz

A Mano (By Hand) stocks fine home furnishings and accessories crafted by European artisans.

🔲 C3 ✉ 1677 Wisconsin Avenue NW ☎ 202/298-7200 🕓 Mon–Sat 10–6, Sun 12–5 🚇 Foggy Bottom, then 15-min walk

AMERICAN HOLIDAY

iloveah.com

From candles to a Mason jar for every occasion and eye-catching vases to chic throws and cushions, this little shop is a mine of stylish gift ideas.

🔲 D4 ✉ 1319 Wisconsin Avenue NW ☎ 202/684-2790 🕓 Mon–Fri 10–7, Sat 10–8, Sun 10–6 🚇 Foggy Bottom, then 15-min walk

ANTHROPOLOGIE

anthropologie.com

Anthropologie is a magnet of shabby chic that sells women's clothing and accessories, homeware and stationery.

🔲 C4 ✉ 3222 M Street NW ☎ 202/337-1363 🕓 Mon–Sat 10–9, Sun 11–7 🚇 Foggy Bottom, then 15-min walk

BLUE MERCURY

bluemercury.com

High-end beauty shop from husband and wife team Barry and Marla Beck. This branch also offers spa services.

SECRET ALLEY

Down a cobblestone side street is Georgetown's design district, Cady's Alley, whose high-end home furnishing and fashion designers complement the local antiques stores. The historic shops open onto a quaint courtyard where Leopold's Kafe and Konditorei (▷ 80) offers a selection of delicious Austrian-inspired gastronomic delights.

🔲 D4 ✉ 3059 M Street NW ☎ 202/965-1300 🕓 Mon–Sat 10–9, Sun 11–6 🚇 Foggy Bottom, then 15-min walk

BRIDGE STREET BOOKS

bridgestreetbooks.com

A quintessential book store, this charming row house contains a good collection of books, with a particularly good section on poetry.

🔲 D4 ✉ 2814 Pennsylvania Avenue NW ☎ 202/965-5200 🕓 Mon–Thu 11–9, Fri–Sat 11–10, Sun 12–6 🚇 Foggy Bottom, then 10-min walk

THE FRYE COMPANY

Make your way here for high-quality men's and women's boots, shoes and bags, along with leather goods, accessories and clothes.

🔲 C4 ✉ 1066 Wisconsin Avenue NW ☎ 2202/337-3793 🕓 Mon–Sat 10–8, Sun 11–6 🚇 Foggy Bottom, then 15-min walk

HU'S SHOES

husonline.com

On the absolute front edge of fashion, hu's shoes prides itself on its collection of women's shoes and accessories rarely found outside of New York, Paris or Milan.

🔲 D4 ✉ 3005 M Street NW (also 2906 M Street) ☎ 202/342-0202 🕓 Mon–Sat 10–7, Sun 12–5 🚇 Foggy Bottom, then 15-min walk

JEAN PIERRE ANTIQUES

There's no need to go to France for that special piece: Enjoy this Georgetown shop that finds and supplies antique furniture to well-heeled locals and famous visitors.

🔲 D4 ✉ 2601 P Street NW ☎ 202/337-1731 🕓 Mon–Fri 11–5, Sat–Sun 12–5 🚇 Dupont Circle, then 15-min walk

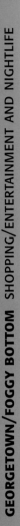

JUST PAPER AND TEA

justpaperandtea.com

Just Paper and Tea sells just what is says. It's home to a large selection of fine paper and quality stationery and a wide range of loose and bagged artisan teas.

➕ C4 ✉ 3232 P Street NW ☎ 202-333-9141 🕔 Tue–Sat 10–5 🚌 D.C. Circulator bus

KIEHL'S

kiehls.com

Kiehl's has had a strong following for its quality skincare products since opening as an apothecary in 1851.

➕ D4 ✉ 3110 M Street NW ☎ 202-333-5101 🕔 Mon–Sat 10–7, Sun 12–6 🚇 Foggy Bottom, then 10-min walk

LILLY PULITZER

lillypulitzer.com

This is the place for brightly-hued dresses, swimwear and accessories. Styles are inspired by the fashions of Palm Beach, Florida.

➕ C4 ✉ 1079 Wisconsin Avenue NW ☎ 202-971-8212 🕔 Mon–Sat 10–8, Sun 11–6 🚇 Foggy Bottom, then 15-min walk

VILLAGE ART AND CRAFT

bellydancethings.com

India is the source for the pashminas, scarves, silks, sarees, jewelry and housewares on display here.

➕ D4 ✉ 1625 Wisconsin Avenue NW ☎ 202-333-1968 🕔 Mon–Sat 10–7, Sun 11–5 🚇 Foggy Bottom, then 15-min walk

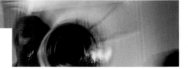

Entertainment and Nightlife

BIG WHEEL BIKES

bigwheelbikes.com

Road bikes, mountain bikes, hybrids—rent a bike to suit your riding style at this location next to the C&O Canal bike path.

➕ C4 ✉ 1034 33rd Street NW ☎ 202-337-0254 🕔 Tue–Sun 10–6 🚇 Foggy Bottom, then 15-min walk

BIRRERIA PARADISO

eatyourpizza.com

Downstairs from Pizzeria Paradiso (▷ 80), this temple of beer has 16 of the world's finest varieties on tap and 80 in bottles. Many of the beers have a high ABV so do take note.

➕ C4 ✉ 3282 M Street NW ☎ 202-337-1245 🕔 Mon–Thu 11.30–10, Fri–Sat 11.30–11, Sun 12–10 🚇 Foggy Bottom

BLUES ALLEY

bluesalley.com

A legendary jazz club, Blues Alley was founded in 1965 and made famous by the likes of Dizzy Gillespie and Charlie Byrd. It regularly pulls in the nation's top acts.

➕ C4 ✉ Rear of 1073 Wisconsin Avenue NW ☎ 202-337-4141 🕔 Daily 6pm–12.30am 🚇 Foggy Bottom, then 15-min walk

HALF-PRICE TICKETS

TICKETplace (ticketplace.org) offers same-day half-price tickets (available online only) for a variety of shows around town. There is a variable service charge, so be sure to check what you are paying. Many theaters also sell discounted preview week or last-minute tickets.

DEGREES

ritzcarlton.com

This elegant watering hole in the lobby of the Ritz-Carlton draws well-dressed patrons. You'll be served great cocktails while sitting at the sleek black slate bar.
➕ C4 ✉ 3100 South Street NW ☎ 202/912-4146 🕐 Daily breakfast, lunch, dinner 🚇 Foggy Bottom, then 15-min walk

GEORGETOWN PIANO BAR

georgetownpianobar.com

A cherry-red grand piano is the center-piece of this friendly, casual spot in the heart of Georgetown. Sing along to the choices of the in-house pianist or step up to the mic yourself.
➕ C4 ✉ 3287 M Street, NW ☎ 202/337-1871 🕐 Mon–Fri 5–2, Sat–Sun 5–3. Piano music daily starting at 7pm 🚇 Foggy Bottom, then 15-min walk

GYPSY SALLY'S

gypsysallys.com

Tucked under the Whitehurst Freeway, this is a comfortable and friendly music venue that also serves food and drink.
➕ C4 ✉ 3401 K Street NW ☎ 202/333-7700 🕐 Tue–Sat 6pm till late 🚇 Foggy Bottom, then 10-min walk

JOHN F. KENNEDY CENTER

D.C.'s top spot for renowned performers (▷ 74).

MARTIN'S TAVERN

martinstavern.com

This distinguished but unpretentious saloon was a favorite of the young JFK and Jackie. Dark leather booths are named after famous former diners.
➕ C4 ✉ 1264 Wisconsin Avenue NW ☎ 202/333-7370 🕐 Mon–Thu 11am–1.30am, Fri 11am–2.30am, Sat 8am–2.30am, Sun 8am–1.30am 🚇 Foggy Bottom, then 15-min walk

SEQUOIA

arkrestaurants.com/sequoia

On the waterfront with a lovely view over the river, the bar at Sequoia is a popular place for a drink.
➕ D5 ✉ 3000 K Street NW ☎ 202/944-4200 🕐 Daily brunch, lunch, dinner 🚇 Foggy Bottom, then 15-min walk

SUSHERIA

susheriadc.com

Susheria offers sushi and ceviche, as well as specialty cocktails. The interesting menu fuses Japanese and Peruvian cuisine.
➕ C5 ✉ 3101 K Street NW ☎ 202/333-2006 🕐 Daily 11am–late 🚇 Foggy Bottom, then 15-min walk

THOMPSON BOAT CENTER

thompsonboatcenter.com

See the city from the water and rent a canoe, rowing shell or kayak.
➕ D5 ✉ 2900 Virginia Avenue NW ☎ 202/333-9543 🕐 Rentals mid-Mar to Oct daily 8–6 🚇 Foggy Bottom, then 15-min walk

THE TOMBS

tombs.com

This subterranean bar, adorned with vintage crew prints and oars, is popular among students.
➕ B4 ✉ 1226 36th Street NW ☎ 202/337-6668 🕐 Check website for opening times 🚇 Foggy Bottom, then 15-min walk

---

BARBECUE BATTLE

One weekend every June barbecuers from around the country gather on Pennsylvania Avenue NW, between 9th and 14th streets, to face off. But it's not just about the flames. Entertainment includes live rock, jazz and blues music acts and cooking demonstrations.

Where to Eat

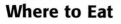

PRICES

Prices are approximate, based on a
3-course meal for one person.

$$$	over $50
$$	$30–$50
$	under $30

BOURBON STEAK ($$$)

bourbonsteakdc.com

Dry-aged beef poached in butter prior to grilling is the star at this steakhouse in the Four Seasons Hotel. Great fish dishes, a range of cocktails and attentive service are more reasons to come.
➕ C4 ✉ 2800 Pennsylvania Avenue NW
☎ 202/342-0444 🕔 Mon–Fri 11.30–2.30, Sun–Thu 6–10, Fri 6–10.30, Sat 5.30–10.30
🚇 Foggy Bottom

CHEZ BILLY SUD ($$$)

chezbillysud.com

The draws at this charming intimate bistro are the handcrafted cocktails and expertly prepared dishes inspired by the cuisine of Southern France.
➕ C4 ✉ 1039 31st Street NW ☎ 202/965-2606 🕔 Daily dinner, lunch Tue–Fri, Sat–Sun brunch 🚇 Foggy Bottom, then 15-min walk

DOG TAG BAKERY ($)

dogtagbakery.org

Coffee, pastries and sandwiches are prepared in-house by wounded veterans who are completing a Georgetown University work-study program.
➕ B4 ✉ 3206 Grace Street NW ☎ 202/527-9388 🕔 Mon–Fri 7–6, Sat–Sun 8–6 🚇 Foggy Bottom, then 15-min walk

FIOLA MARE ($$$)

fiolamaredc.com

"The city's most sumptuous spot for seafood," said The Washington Post. That and handmade pastas, along with the beautiful decor, have made this one of D.C.'s in-demand dining rooms.
➕ D5 ✉ 3050 K Street NW ☎ 202/525-1402 🕔 Sat 11.30–2, Sun 11–2; Sun–Thu 5–10, Fri–Sat 5–10.30 🚇 Foggy Bottom, then 15-min walk

LEOPOLD'S KAFE AND KONDITOREI ($$)

kafeleopolds.com

This Austrian café offers dishes ranging from schnitzel to salads and is well-known for its huge pastry selection.
➕ C4 ✉ 3315 Cadys Alley NW ☎ 202/965-6005 🕔 Sun–Tue 8am–10pm, Wed 8am–11pm, Thu–Sat 8am–midnight
🚇 Foggy Bottom, then 15-min walk

MISS SAIGON ($–$$)

ms-saigonus.com

An extensive menu of traditional Vietnamese dishes is expertly prepared at this popular, atmospheric restaurant.
➕ D4 ✉ 3057 M Street NW ☎ 202/333-5545 🕔 Sun–Thu 11.30–10, Fri–Sat 11.30–10.30 🚇 Foggy Bottom, then 15-min walk

PIZZERIA PARADISO ($)

eatyourpizza.com

The stone, wood-burning oven is the heart of this restaurant, which produces the best Neapolitan pizza in town.
➕ C4 ✉ 3282 M Street NW ☎ 202/337-1245 🕔 Mon–Thu 11.30–10, Fri–Sat 11.30–11, Sun 12–10 🚇 Foggy Bottom, then 15-min walk

SWEETGREEN ($)

sweetgreen.com

People come here for the delicious salads that are made using quality local organic ingredients.
➕ C4 ✉ 2221 I Street NW ☎ 202/507-8357 🕔 Daily 10.30–10.30 🚇 Foggy Bottom, then 15-min walk

Northwest Washington

Mostly residential, Northwest Washington is home to shady streets, embassies and the expansive Rock Creek Park. With more than its fair share of bars and restaurants, it's also a popular nighttime destination.

Top 25

National Zoological Park **84**

Phillips Collection **85**

Rock Creek Park **86**

Washington National Cathedral **87**

More to See **88**

Walk **89**

Shopping **90**

Entertainment and Nightlife **92**

Where to Eat **93**

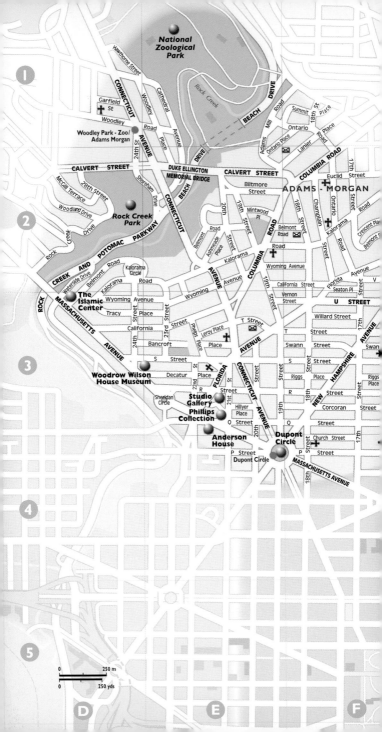

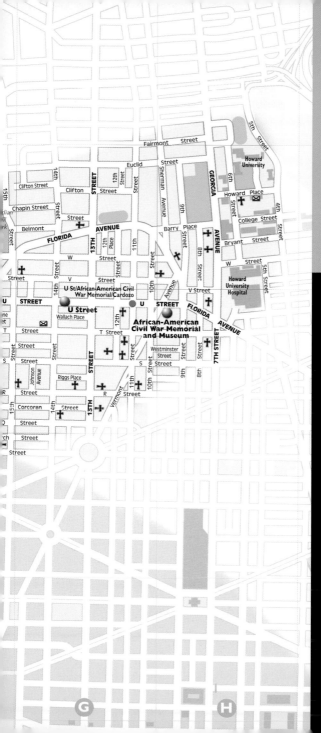

Fairmont   Street

Euclid   Street

Clifton Street   Clifton   Street

Chapin Street   Street

Belmont   Street

FLORIDA

W   Street

V   Street

U St/African-American Civil
War Memorial/Cardozo

U Street

Wallach Place

T   Street

Johnson Avenue

Riggs Place

Corcoran   Street

Howard
University

Howard Place   Street

College Street

Bryant   Street

W   Street

Howard
University
Hospital

Barry   Place

V Street

U   STREET

African-American
Civil War Memorial
and Museum

Westminster
Street

FLORIDA   AVENUE

7TH STREET

National Zoological Park

TOP 25

Playful orangutans draw the crowds at the National Zoological Park

THE BASICS

nationalzoo.si.edu

✚ E1

✉ 3001 Connecticut Avenue NW

☎ 202/633-4888

🕓 Grounds: mid-Mar to Sep daily 8–7; Oct to mid-Mar 8–5. Animal buildings: mid-Mar to Sep daily 9–6; Oct to mid-Mar 9–4

♿ Free. Parking charge

⚅ Excellent

🍴 Snack bars, cafés

Ⓜ Woodley Park–Zoo

HIGHLIGHTS

● Amazonia
● Orangutans on the "O line"
● Bird House
● Elephants
● Lions, tigers and cheetahs
● Kids' Farm
● Daily walking tours

Founded in 1889, this 163-acre (66ha) park, one of America's finest zoos, is home to more than 2,700 animals from almost 400 species. Come here to see seals swim, monkeys swing and meerkats dart.

Before elephants and donkeys A national zoo was the vision of William Hornaday, who was a taxidermist at the Smithsonian. Hornaday opened a trial zoo, packed with animals, right outside the Smithsonian Castle on the Mall. Not surprisingly, Congress soon approved a site a little farther away in Rock Creek Park, which the zoo still calls home. Plans for the spot were drawn up by Hornaday and Frederick Law Olmsted, Jr., son of the designer of Central Park in New York. When Hornaday was not chosen to be the first director of the zoo, he left and founded the Bronx Zoo.

America's park As part of a cooperative breeding agreement with the China Wildlife Conservation Association panda cubs born at the zoo move to China when they reach the age of four. Resident pandas Tian Tian, Mei Xiang and Bei Bei can, however, be watched on the Giant Panda Cam as they chomp on bamboo, play in trees and tumble in the grass. Visitors also come to see the big cats, the "O line," which allows orangutans to swing freely, Amazonia and the Reptile Discovery Center. The bison were reintroduced to celebrate the zoo's 125th anniversary in 2014.

THE BASICS

phillipscollection.org

🔼 E3

✉ 1600 21st Street NW

☎ 202/387-2151

🕐 Tue–Sat 10–5 (Thu until 8.30), Sun 12–6.30. Closed public hols

💲 Permanent collection: free weekdays, expensive Sat–Sun. Temporary exhibitions: moderate

♿ Excellent

🍴 Café

Ⓜ Dupont Circle

❓ There is a full program of guided tours around a particular theme or exhibition as well as daily self-guided visits. The annual Phillips Music Seasons has been a tradition since 1941 (advance booking advisable)

This collection in the former house of Duncan Phillips was America's first museum of modern art. It is world-renowned for its fine collection of Impressionist and Postimpressionist paintings and other artworks.

Duncan Phillips After the premature death of his father and brother, Phillips established a gallery in their honor in a room of his Georgian Revival home, and it was opened to the public in 1921. Over the years, Phillips and his wife Marjorie, a painter, continued to buy art with a keen eye. Phillips believed strongly in an art lineage—that artists were clearly influenced by their predecessors as they were in turn by those who came before them. The size of his collection grew to more than 3,000 works, including some that were considered risqué at the time—Georgia O'Keeffe, Mark Rothko and Pierre Bonnard. They also acquired Auguste Renoir's much admired *Luncheon of the Boating Party*. In 1930, Phillips moved out of the grand building and the collection took over. However, he continued to direct the gallery until his death in 1966.

Current works The permanent collection contains works by Piet Mondrian, Paul Klee, Pablo Picasso, Monet, Degas, Matisse, van Gogh, Cézanne and many well-known American artists. It holds a large collection of works by Arthur Dove (1880–1946), regarded as the first American abstract painter.

HIGHLIGHTS

● *Luncheon of the Boating Party*, Auguste Renoir
● *The Rothko Room*, Mark Rothko
● *Repentant St. Peter*, El Greco
● *Entrance to the Public Garden at Arles*, Vincent van Gogh
● *Dancers at the Barre*, Edgar Degas
● *The Migration Series*, Jacob Lawrence

Rock Creek Park

TOP
25

Rock Creek Park in fall
(left); Rock Creek (right)

THE BASICS

nps.gov/rocr

🔲 D2

✉ Nature Center, 5200
Glover Road NW

☎ Park and Nature
Center 202/895-6000

🕐 Nature Center:
Wed–Sun 9–5. Grounds:
daylight hours

✋ Free

🚇 Friendship Heights
then E-2 or E-3 bus

HIGHLIGHTS

● Rock Creek Parkway
● Running and biking trails
● Carter Barron
Amphitheater
● Nature Center and
Planetarium
● Peirce Mill
● Extensive hiking trails

A geological rift that slices through northwest D.C., Rock Creek Park is one of the few metropolitan parks to be shaped mainly by its geology, not the work of man. It's a favorite escape for the city's residents.

Park of presidents In 1890, President Benjamin Harrison (1833–1901) signed a bill establishing Rock Creek Park as one of the first national parks. The area, over 1,700 acres (687ha), was acquired for a little more than $1 million. While in office, President Theodore Roosevelt, an avid naturalist, would often spend his afternoons hiking in unmarked sections of the park with the French Ambassador, making sure to return after dark so that his appearance "would scandalize no one." Rock Creek Parkway, on the National Registry of Historic Places, was built from 1923 to 1936. During his presidency, Woodrow Wilson would have his driver drop him off in the park with Edith Bolling Galt, whom he would later marry, and then pick them up farther down the road.

Playground of Washingtonians At twice the size of Central Park, Rock Creek Park has enough room for everyone. A paved bike trail leads from the Lincoln Memorial all the way to Maryland, and Beach Drive north of Military Road is closed to motor traffic on the weekends during the day. The park is full of hiking trails and picnic areas, and has a golf course, tennis courts and horse center.

The Cathedral, seen from the Bishop's Garden (left); interior of the cathedral (right)

TOP 25

Washington National Cathedral

The soaring Gothic cathedral is often the setting for national commemorations in times of celebration, crisis and sorrow. Its official name is the Cathedral Church of Saint Peter and Saint Paul in the City and Diocese of Washington, but everyone knows it as the National Cathedral.

Presidential past Three U.S. presidents have had their state funeral here: Dwight Eisenhower, Ronald Reagan and Gerald Ford. Several others were honored with prayer or memorial services after their deaths, including John F. Kennedy, Franklin D. Roosevelt, Calvin Coolidge and Harry S. Truman. Fittingly, a number of presidential inauguration prayer services have been held here, including one for Donald Trump in 2017.

Solid foundation The first foundation stone—made of Indiana limestone—was laid in 1907, and the last wasn't set in place until 83 years later, in 1990. Four architects and thousands of masons, sculptors and other workers labored to create the majestic Gothic structure whose tallest tower reaches 300ft (90m). In 2011, the cathedral sustained major damage when a 5.8 magnitude earthquake shook the city and the surrounding area. Stones on several pinnacles broke off, gargoyles and other carvings were damaged, and falling stone punched a hole in the roof. The cathedral was closed for several months after the earthquake and repairs, which could take up to 15 years, have been estimated at $26 million.

THE BASICS

cathedral.org
+ B1
✉ 3101 Wisconsin Avenue NW
☎ 202/537-6200
🕐 Mon–Fri 10–5.30, Sat 10–4.30; last entry 30 mins before close. Sun services
👤 Moderate
🚇 Dupont Circle, then N2, N3, N4 or N6 bus
❓ Behind the scenes tours daily (check website)—advance booking advisable. Full concert program

HIGHLIGHTS

● Exterior gargoyles
● Bell tower with two sets of bells (53-bell carillon and 10-bell peal)
● Pulpit carved from stones from Canterbury Cathedral
● The Great Organ, installed in 1938
● Pilgrim Observation Gallery
● Sculpture of Darth Vader on top of northwest tower (binoculars required)

NORTHWEST WASHINGTON TOP 25

More to See

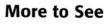

AFRICAN-AMERICAN CIVIL WAR MEMORIAL AND MUSEUM

afroamcivilwar.org

This museum tells the story of the 209,145 African-Americans who fought to abolish slavery in the American Civil War. Edward Hamilton's bronze memorial, across the street from the museum, was dedicated in 1998.

➕ H3 ✉ 1925 Vermont Avenue NW ☎ 202/667-2667 🕐 Mon 10–5, Tue–Fri 10–6.30, Sat 10–4, Sun 12–4; Memorial daily 24 hours 🚇 U Street/African-American Civil War Memorial/Cardozo 🎫 Free

ANDERSON HOUSE

societyofthecincinnati.org

A visit to this 1905 Beaux Arts mansion provides a glimpse into the Gilded Age life of its art-collecting, patriotic owners.

➕ E3 ✉ 2118 Massachusetts Avenue NW 🕐 Tue–Sat 10–4, Sun 12–4 🚇 Dupont Circle 🎫 Free

BISHOP'S GARDEN

cathedral.org/gardens

Winding paths, perennial borders and rustic stone walls make the Washington National Cathedral garden an oasis from urban bustle.

➕ B1 ✉ Wisconsin and Massachusetts avenues NW ☎ 202/537-2937 🕐 Daily dawn–dusk 🚇 Dupont Circle, then N2, N3, N4 or N6 bus 🎫 Free

DUPONT CIRCLE

Dupont is a dynamic pedestrian-friendly neighborhood, hosting one of the city's year-round farmers' market. In warmer months, the grassy areas team with people.

➕ E4 🚇 Dupont Circle

THE ISLAMIC CENTER

theislamiccenter.com

Calls to the faithful emanate from the 162ft (49m) minaret of this mosque, built in 1957. The inside is beautifully adorned.

➕ D3 ✉ 2551 Massachusetts Avenue NW ☎ 202/332-8343 🕐 Cultural Center: daily 10–5; mosque: between prayer times. Tours available 🚇 Dupont Circle

STUDIO GALLERY

studiogallerydc.com

Artists in the D.C. area contribute to the changing exhibitions of contemporary art showcased here. The gallery was set up in 1956 by artist Jennie Lea Knight and has been owned by artists ever since.

➕ E3 ✉ 2108 R Street NW ☎ 202/232-8734 🕐 Wed–Fri 1–6, Sat 11–6 🚇 Dupont Circle

U STREET

U Street used to be a real draw for jazz musicians and a hub of D.C.'s black community. Smart apartment buildings are interspersed with live music venues and bars.

➕ G3 ✉ U Street between 10th and 15th streets 🚇 U Street/African-American Civil War Memorial/Cardozo

WOODROW WILSON HOUSE MUSEUM

woodrowwilsonhouse.org

Woodrow Wilson and his wife lived here from 1921, after he left the White House, until his death in 1924. The museum reflects life during this time.

➕ D/E3 ✉ 2340 S Street NW ☎ 202/387-4062 🕐 Visited on bookable group tours; times vary according to season 🚇 Dupont Circle 🎫 Inexpensive

Cosmopolitan Washington

Dupont's tree-lined streets and Circle offer a glimpse of both young D.C. and elegant, old-fashioned architecture.

DISTANCE: 2.5 miles (4km) **ALLOW:** 1 hour 30 minutes

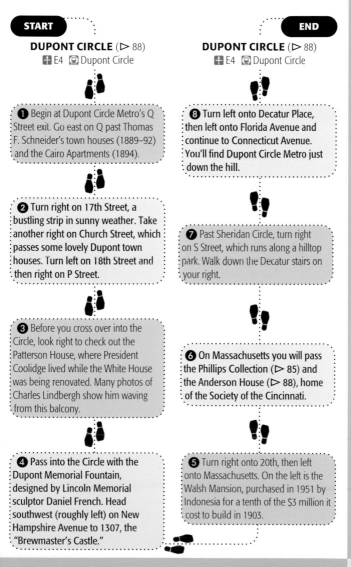

START

DUPONT CIRCLE (▷ 88)
🚇 E4 Ⓜ Dupont Circle

① Begin at Dupont Circle Metro's Q Street exit. Go east on Q past Thomas F. Schneider's town houses (1889–92) and the Cairo Apartments (1894).

② Turn right on 17th Street, a bustling strip in sunny weather. Take another right on Church Street, which passes some lovely Dupont town houses. Turn left on 18th Street and then right on P Street.

③ Before you cross over into the Circle, look right to check out the Patterson House, where President Coolidge lived while the White House was being renovated. Many photos of Charles Lindbergh show him waving from this balcony.

④ Pass into the Circle with the Dupont Memorial Fountain, designed by Lincoln Memorial sculptor Daniel French. Head southwest (roughly left) on New Hampshire Avenue to 1307, the "Brewmaster's Castle."

END

DUPONT CIRCLE (▷ 88)
🚇 E4 Ⓜ Dupont Circle

⑧ Turn left onto Decatur Place, then left onto Florida Avenue and continue to Connecticut Avenue. You'll find Dupont Circle Metro just down the hill.

⑦ Past Sheridan Circle, turn right on S Street, which runs along a hilltop park. Walk down the Decatur stairs on your right.

⑥ On Massachusetts you will pass the Phillips Collection (▷ 85) and the Anderson House (▷ 88), home of the Society of the Cincinnati.

⑤ Turn right onto 20th, then left onto Massachusetts. On the left is the Walsh Mansion, purchased in 1951 by Indonesia for a tenth of the $3 million it cost to build in 1903.

Shopping

BETSY FISHER

betsyfisher.com

Carrying designers such as Nanette Lapore and Diane von Furstenberg, along with a few local designers, Betsy Fisher attracts women of all ages.

🔲 F4 ✉ 1224 Connecticut Avenue NW ☎ 202/785-1975 🕔 Mon–Fri 10–7, Sat 10–6, Sun 1–5 🚇 Dupont Circle

BLUE MERCURY

bluemercury.com

Aside from its hard-to-match selection of hair and skin-care products, Blue Mercury also sells Diptyque candles.

🔲 E3 ✉ 1619 Connecticut Avenue NW ☎ 202/462-1300 🕔 Mon–Sat 10–8, Sun 11–6 🚇 Dupont Circle

CALVERT WOODLEY LIQUORS

calvertwoodley.com

Calvert Woodley stocks D.C.'s largest selection of wine, as well as a range of fantastic cheese.

🔲 D1 ✉ 4339 Connecticut Avenue NW ☎ 202/966-4400 🕔 Mon–Fri 10–8.30, Sat 9.30–8.30, Sun 10.30–5 🚇 Woodley Park-Zoo

GLEN'S GARDEN MARKET

glensgardenmarket.com

The deli here puts the emphasis on small, responsible brands, selling only regionally grown and made foodstuffs.

🔲 E3 ✉ 2001 S Street NW ☎ 202/588-5698 🕔 Mon–Fri 8am–10pm, Sat 9am–10pm, Sun 9–9 🚇 Dupont Circle

GOOD WOOD

goodwooddc.com

This friendly U Street shop carries high-quality, reasonably priced furniture, homeware and vintage jewelry.

🔲 G3 ✉ 1428 U Street NW ☎ 202/986-3640 🕔 Mon–Sat 12–7, Sun 12–5 🚇 U Street/African-American Civil War Memorial/Cardozo

HANA JAPANESE MARKET

Customers to this snug shop will find a wide variety of Japanese foods, both fresh and frozen.

🔲 E3 ✉ 2000 17th Street NW ☎ 202/939-8854 🕔 Daily 10–8 🚇 U Street/African-American Civil War Memorial/Cardozo

HEMPHILL FINE ARTS

hemphillfinearts.com

This large gallery stocks an impressive array of works by American artists responding to socially relevant subjects.

🔲 G4 ✉ 1515 14th Street NW, 3rd floor ☎ 202/234-5601 🕔 Tue–Fri 10–5 or by appointment 🚇 U Street/African-American Civil War Memorial/Cardozo

JENNI BICK CUSTOM JOURNALS

jennibick.com

This stationery store is packed with unique journals, notebooks, pens and anything else a scribe might want.

🔲 E3 ✉ 1300 Connecticut Avenue NW ☎ 202/721-0246 🕔 Mon–Sat 10–7, Sun 12–6 🚇 Dupont Circle

KRAMERBOOKS AND AFTERWORDS CAFÉ

kramers.com

This landmark bookstore/bar/brunch spot/late-night hangout is always buzzing with book-lovers and diners.

🔲 E3 ✉ 1517 Connecticut Avenue NW ☎ 202/387-1400 🕔 Mon–Thu 7.30am–1am, Fri–Sat 7.30am–3am 🚇 Dupont Circle

MEEPS

meepsdc.com

Meeps sells well-priced vintage clothing from the 1950s onward.

🔲 F3 ✉ 2104 18th Street NW ☎ 202/265-6546 🕔 Sun–Mon 12–7, Tue–Sat 12–8 🚇 U Street/African-American Civil War Memorial/Cardozo

MISS PIXIE'S

misspixies.com

Stocked with low-price antiques and vintage home furnishings, Miss Pixie's is a popular place to browse.

➕ G2 ✉ 1626 14th Street NW ☎ 202/232-8171 ⏰ Daily 11–7 Ⓜ U Street/African-American Civil War Memorial/Cardozo

PROPER TOPPER

propertopper.com

Fashionable headwear is the main draw, but there's also a great selection of quirky accessories, clothing, books, home decor and a children's section.

➕ F4 ✉ 1350 Connecticut Avenue NW ✉ 202/842-3055 ⏰ Mon–Fri 11–7, Sat 10–6, Sun 11–5 Ⓜ Dupont Circle

RIZIK'S

riziks.com

From evening wear through bridal wear to casual day clothes and coats and jackets, Rizik's has led the evolution of couture fashion in Washington.

➕ F4 ✉ 1100 Connecticut Avenue NW ✉ 202/223-4050 ⏰ Mon–Sat 9–6 Ⓜ Farragut North

SECOND STORY BOOKS

secondstorybooks.com

If used books are your passion, then you should come here. If you don't find your treasure in store, it may well be in Second Story's large warehouse.

➕ E4 ✉ 2000 P Street NW ☎ 202/659-8884 ⏰ Daily 10–10 Ⓜ Dupont Circle

SECONDI

secondi.com

With a sunny and spacious store and caring staff, this is Washington's top stop for designer consignment. Brands include Chanel, Kate Space, Marc Jacobs, Prada and Louis Vuitton.

➕ E3 ✉ 1702 Connecticut Avenue NW, 2nd floor ☎ 202/667-1122 ⏰ Mon–Tue 11–6, Wed–Fri 11–7, Sat 11–6, Sun 1–5 Ⓜ Dupont Circle

SHOP MADE IN DC

shopmadeindc.com

Shop Made In DC is a retail initiative with a mission to support and grow the city's creatives and crafting community. Check website for events program.

➕ E3 ✉ 1710 Connecticut Avenue NW ☎ No phone ⏰ Mon–Sat 10–8, Sun 10–7 Ⓜ Dupont Circle

SMASH RECORDS

smashrecords.com

Vinyl, vintage clothes and a cool vibe. Knowledgeable staff are on hand to help you find your way around everything from hip-hop to hard-core punk.

➕ F2 ✉ 2314 18th Street NW, 2nd floor ☎ 202/387-6274 ⏰ Mon–Thu 12–9, Fri 12–10, Sat 11–10, Sun 12–7 Ⓜ U Street/African-American Civil War Memorial/Cardozo

TABLETOP

tabletopdc.com

Tabletop features sleek retro homewares. Items are well designed, and priced as such, but there is also a bargain area in the back.

➕ E3 ✉ 1608 20th Street NW ☎ 202/387-7117 ⏰ Mon–Sat 11–7, Sun 10–5 Ⓜ Dupont Circle

TINY JEWEL BOX

tinyjewelbox.com

The Rosenheim family sells elegant jewelry and timepieces to visitors and Washingtonians alike, and has been doing so for more than 85 years.

➕ F4 ✉ 11155 Connecticut Avenue NW ☎ 202/393-2747 ⏰ Mon–Sat 10–5.30 Ⓜ Dupont Circle

Entertainment and Nightlife

9:30 CLUB

930.com

See the most popular non-stadium acts take the stage at this well-designed club that's been around for over 35 years.

🏠 H2 ✉ 815 V Street NW ☎ 202/265-0930 🕐 Hours vary, check online 🚇 U Street/African-American Civil War Memorial/Cardozo

BLACK JACK

blackjackdc.com

This lively and upbeat bar offers pizza, inventive cocktails, as well as a bocce court (a ball game similar to bowls or pétanque).

🏠 G3 ✉ 1612 14th Street NW ☎ 202/319-1612 🕐 Tue–Thu 6pm–12.30am, Fri 5pm–1.30am, Sat 3pm–1.30am, Sun 3pm–12.30am 🚇 Dupont Circle, then 10-min walk

CAFÉ CITRON

cafecitrondc.com

Live Latin music and well-priced mojitos keep this spot popular. It also serves sharing platters and pitchers.

🏠 F4 ✉ 1343 Connecticut Avenue NW ☎ 202/530-8844 🕐 Wed–Thu 5pm–2am, Fri–Sat 5pm–3am 🚇 Dupont Circle ❓ Dance classes (free) several nights per week

CHI-CHA LOUNGE

chichaloungedc.com

A plush lounge filled with sofas, Chi-Cha offers live Latin jazz, tapas, a tasty namesake drink and hookahs.

🏠 F3 ✉ 1624 U Street NW ☎ 202/906-9417 🕐 Sun–Thu 4pm–11.30pm, Fri–Sat 4pm–1.30am 🚇 U Street/African-American Civil War Memorial/Cardozo/Dupont Circle

EIGHTEENTH STREET LOUNGE

This multilevel house party is popular among Washington's most glamorous (you'll need to dress well). With five areas to choose from, the interior is a dark, candlelit affair, while in the summer the deck bar is always bustling.

🏠 F4 ✉ 1212 18th Street NW ☎ 202/696-0210 🕐 Tue–Sun, check online for more details 🚇 Dupont Circle

SALOON

There's a no TV, no standing and no cell phones at the bar policy here, but regulars find the beer list and the conversation inviting.

🏠 E3 ✉ 1205 U Street NW ☎ 202/462-2640 🕐 Call for daily opening and closing times 🚇 U Street/African-American Civil War Memorial/Cardozo

U STREET MUSIC HALL

ustreetmusichall.com

This is a club designed for those who love dancing. It has one of the city's best sound systems and there are no seated performances.

🏠 G3 ✉ 1115 U Street NW ☎ 202/588-1889 🕐 Hours vary, check online 🚇 U Street/African-American Civil War Memorial/Cardozo

VEGAS LOUNGE

newvegasloungedc.com

Classic and modern-day rhythm and blues has been keeping fans satisfied for 50 years.

🏠 G4 ✉ 1415 P Street NW ☎ 202/483-3971 🕐 Fri–Sat 9pm (open), 10pm (shows start) 🚇 Dupont Circle, then 10-min walk ❓ Guest bands 1st and 3rd Thu at 8pm

H STREET NE

There's plenty going on in the evening here. Go for tequila and mini golf at H Street County Club, German beers at Biergarten Haus, live music at Rock and Roll Hotel, craft cocktails at Haymaker Bar, DJs and dinner at Smith Commons, and beer and shots courtesy of The Pug.

Where to Eat

PRICES	
Prices are approximate, based on a 3-course meal for one person.	
$$$	over $50
$$	$30–$50
$	under $30

AMSTERDAM FALAFELSHOP ($)

falafelshop.com

Falafel and fries may be the only thing on the menu here, but dozens of fresh toppings make the difference.

➕ F2 ✉ 1830 14th Street NW ☎ 202/234-1969 🕐 Daily 11am–very late 🚇 Woodley Park–Zoo, then 10-min walk

BEN'S CHILI BOWL ($)

benschilibowl.com

This U Street institution sells burgers, chili dogs and fries to a late-night crowd.

➕ G3 ✉ 1213 U Street NW ☎ 202/667-0909 🕐 Mon–Thu 6am–2am, Fri–Sat 6am–4am, Sun 11am–midnight 🚇 U Street/African-American Civil War Memorial/Cardozo

BRIXTON ($)

brixtondc.com

A British-style pub with regular happy hours, the Brixton serves pub grub with a twist. The Lodge Bar has brick-lined walls and a welcoming fireplace. The roof deck has great views.

➕ H3 ✉ 901 U Street NW ☎ 202/560-5045 🕐 Mon–Fri 5pm–late, Sat 1pm–3am, Sun 1pm–late 🚇 U Street/African-American Civil War Memorial/Cardozo

BUSBOYS AND POETS ($–$$)

busboysandpoets.com

D.C.'s favorite coffee shop, bookstore, restaurant, art gallery and performance space. Vegan options on the menu.

➕ G3 ✉ 2021 14th Street NW ☎ 202/387-7638 🕐 Sun 8am–midnight, Mon–Thu 7am–midnight, Fri 7am–1am, Sat 8am–1am 🚇 U Street/African-American Civil War Memorial/Cardozo

LE DIPLOMATE ($$$)

lediplomatedc.com

Reservations at this exceptional Parisian-style brasserie have been coveted ever since its critically acclaimed opening.

➕ G3 ✉ 1601 14th Street NW ☎ 202/332-3333 🕐 Daily brunch, lunch, dinner and happy hours 🚇 Dupont Circle, then 10-min walk

HANK'S OYSTER BAR ($$)

hanksoysterbar.com

This lively seafood stop serves up simple yet skillful dishes combining the finest ingredients.

➕ F3 ✉ 1624 Q Street NW ☎ 202/462-4265 🕐 Daily lunch, dinner 🚇 Dupont Circle

INDIQUE ($$)

indique.com

Modern Indian food, a fresh take on the American classics and creative cocktails make up Indique's menu.

➕ Off map at D1 ✉ 3512 Connecticut Avenue NW ☎ 202/244-6600 🕐 Sun 11–3, 5.30–10, Mon–Thu 5–10, Fri 12–3, 5–10.30, Sat 11–3, 5.30–10.30 🚇 Cleveland Park

ETHIOPIAN CUISINE

D.C. is home to the country's largest population of Ethiopian immigrants. Therefore, it's no surprise that the city boasts numerous restaurants serving the colorful, savory cuisine of East Africa, where a meal is always a communal affair: Try Chercher (✉ 1334 9th Street NW ☎ 202/299-9703); Das Ethiopian (✉ 1201 28th Street NW ☎ 202/333-4710); Dukem (✉ 1114–1118 U Street ☎ 202/667-8735); Ethiopic (▷ 106).

KOMI ($$$)

komirestaurant.com

Chef Johnny Monis draws people in with his basic, yet inspired, dishes crafted with exquisite ingredients. The cuisine has Greek influences.

F3 ⊠ 1509 17th Street NW ☎ 202/332-9200 ⏰ Tue–Sat dinner Ⓜ Dupont Circle

LEBANESE TAVERNA ($–$$)

lebanesetaverna.com

Specializing in Lebanese *meze*, this restaurant is known for its warm and welcoming hospitality.

E1 ⊠ 2641 Connecticut Avenue NW ☎ 202/265-8681 ⏰ Sun 12–9, Mon–Thu 11.30–9.30, Fri 11.30–10, Sat 12–10 Ⓜ Woodley Park–Zoo

MEZÈ ($–$$)

mezedc.com

This Turkish spot produces tasty *meze* as well as a menu of substantial fare. There's a selection of mojitos, which you can sample out on the roomy patio.

F2 ⊠ 2437 18th Street NW ☎ 202/797-0017 ⏰ Mon–Thu 4.30pm–1.30am, Fri 4.30pm–2.30am, Sat 11am–2.30am, Sun 11am–1.30am Ⓜ Woodley Park–Zoo

ROOSTER & OWL ($$$)

roosterowl.com

Rooster & Owl invites you to build your own four-course meal under the guidance of culinary professionals merging fine dining and using the best seasonal ingredients.

G3 ⊠ 2436 14th Street NW ☎ 202/813-3976 ⏰ Tue–Sat from 5pm Ⓜ U Street/African-American Civil War Memorial/Cardozo

SATELLITE ($)

satellitedc.com

Satellite is a California-style diner and bar serving beer, pizza and adult milk shakes. It's behind 9:30 Club (▷ 92), so good for a quick bite pre or post gig.

H3 ⊠ 2047 9th Street NW ☎ 202/506-2496 ⏰ Thu–Sun 5pm–close, plus show days at 9:30 Club Ⓜ U Street/African-American Civil War Memorial/Cardozo

SUSHI TARO ($$–$$$)

sushitaro.com

This sushi powerhouse always has three grades of tuna on hand. Reserve a seat at the Omakase counter for an unparalleled dining experience.

F4 ⊠ 1503 17th Street NW ☎ 202/462-8999 ⏰ Mon–Fri 11.30–2, Mon–Sat 5.30–10 Ⓜ Dupont Circle

TAIL UP GOAT ($$)

tailupgoat.com

Crispy salt cod with smoked cauliflower and spicy pork ragu are standout dishes here. The name is a nod to the four-legged ruminants that roam the U.S. Virgin Islands.

F2 ⊠ 1827 Adams Mill Road NW ☎ 202/986-9600 ⏰ Mon–Thu 5.30–10, Fri–Sat 5–10, Sun 11am–1pm, 5–10 Ⓜ Woodley Park–Zoo, then 10-min walk

TEAISM ($)

teaism.com

This simple teahouse offers an eclectic collection of Asian-inspired dishes and good-value Japanese bento boxes.

E3 ⊠ 2009 R Street NW ☎ 202/667-3827 ⏰ Mon–Fri 8am–9pm, Sun 9–9 Ⓜ Dupont Circle

THAI CHEF STREET FOOD ($)

thaichefsushibardc.com

Bangkok-style street food and craft cocktails with a Thai twist.

E3 ⊠ 1712 Connecticut Avenue NW ☎ 202/234-5698 ⏰ Sun–Thu 11.30–10, Fri–Sat 11.30–10.30 Ⓜ Dupont Circle

Farther Afield

Exploring beyond the city center and its residential enclaves is well worth the subway or taxi ride. Historic sites, cultural institutions and acclaimed restaurants abound, as well as great shopping options.

Top 25

Arlington National Cemetery **98**
Frederick Douglass National Historic Site **100**

More to See **102**
Excursions **103**
Shopping **104**
Entertainment and Nightlife **105**
Where to Eat **106**

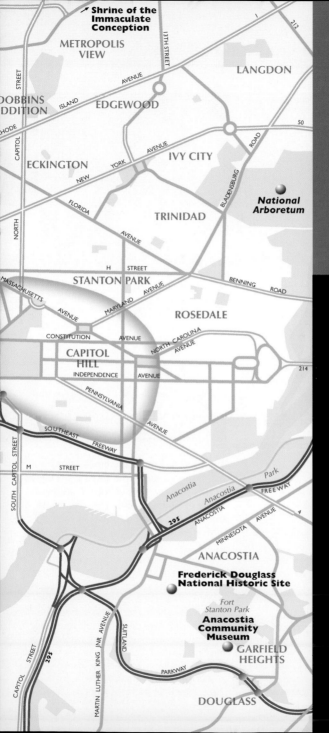

↗ **Shrine of the Immaculate Conception**

METROPOLIS VIEW

LANGDON

DOBBINS ADDITION

ISLAND

EDGEWOOD

13TH STREET

AVENUE

ECKINGTON

YORK AVENUE

IVY CITY

50

RHODE

CAPITOL

NEW

FLORIDA

TRINIDAD

BLADENSBURG ROAD

National Arboretum

NORTH

AVENUE

H STREET

STANTON PARK

BENNING ROAD

MASSACHUSETTS AVENUE

MARYLAND AVENUE

ROSEDALE

CONSTITUTION AVENUE

NORTH CAROLINA AVENUE

CAPITOL HILL

INDEPENDENCE AVENUE

214

PENNSYLVANIA

AVENUE

SOUTH CAPITOL STREET

SOUTHEAST FREEWAY

M STREET

Anacostia

Park

Anacostia

FREEWAY

295

ANACOSTIA AVENUE

4

MINNESOTA AVENUE

ANACOSTIA

Frederick Douglass National Historic Site

Fort Stanton Park

Anacostia Community Museum

SUITLAND

295

MARTIN LUTHER KING JNR AVENUE

CAPITOL STREET

GARFIELD HEIGHTS

PARKWAY

DOUGLASS

Farther Afield

Arlington National Cemetery

HIGHLIGHTS

- Kennedy graves
- Tomb of the Unknowns
- Custis-Lee Mansion
- L'Enfant's grave
- U.S.S. *Maine* Memorial
- Shuttle *Challenger* and *Columbia* memorials
- Astronauts Memorial
- Changing of the Guard at the Tomb of the Unknowns

TIP

● Remember that many visit to pay their respects. Dress appropriately and keep an eye on children.

The national cemetery since 1864, Arlington contains the most visited grave in the country, that of John F. Kennedy. Rows of white crosses commemorate the war dead and national heroes with dignity.

Lest we forget Veterans from every American war are interred here on the land of General Robert E. Lee's (1807–70) Arlington House. Those who fought and died before the Civil War were moved here after 1900. Perhaps the most famous soldiers to be buried here are those that have not yet been named. The Tomb of the Unknowns contains the remains of a World War I, World War II and Korean War soldier. A soldier from the Vietnam War was disinterred in 1998 after DNA evidence identified him.

Clockwise from left: The mast of Battleship Maine surrounded by gravestones in Arlington National Cemetery; Changing of the Guard at the Tomb of the Unknowns; the rooftops of the city of Washington, viewed from the hillside of the cemetery; visitors among the graves and blossom-covered trees

Sentries from the Third U.S. Infantry guard the tomb 24 hours a day and perform the Changing of the Guard ceremony. Other memorials throughout the cemetery commemorate particular events or groups of people, including those killed in the Pentagon on September 11, 2001, and those aboard the Space Shuttle *Columbia* that crashed in 2003.

White markers and a flame Under an eternal flame, John F. Kennedy lies next to his wife, Jacqueline Bouvier Kennedy Onassis, and two of their children who died in infancy. Nearby lies his brother, Robert, whose grave is marked by a simple white cross and a reflecting pool. The Custis-Lee Mansion sits above the Kennedy graves. Just off the house's west corner lies the grave of Pierre L'Enfant, the city's designer.

THE BASICS

arlingtoncemetery.mil

➕ C8

✉ Across Memorial Bridge from Lincoln Memorial

☎ 877/907-8585

🕐 Apr–Sep daily 8–7; Oct–Mar 8–5

🎟 Free

♿ Excellent. Visitors with disabilities may board Arlington National Cemetery tour bus free of charge

🚇 Arlington Cemetery

❓ Tour bus service departs from the Welcome Center 8.30–6 (Oct–Mar). Changing of the Guard: Apr–Sep daily on the half hour; Oct–Mar daily on the hour

Frederick Douglass National Historic Site

The exterior of Cedar Hill (left, right); inside Frederick Douglass's home (below)

THE BASICS

nps.gov/frdo
See map ▷ 97
1411 W Street SE
202/426-5961
Park: Apr–Oct daily 9–5; Nov–Mar 9–4.30. Tours: reserve ahead
Free
Good
Anacostia, then B2 Mt Rainier bus
Daily D.C. Circulator from Union Station to Anacostia
11th Street Bridge to Martin Luther King Avenue, right on W Street

HIGHLIGHTS

● Frederick Douglass's library
● Portraits of Elizabeth Cady Stanton and Susan B. Anthony
● View of Washington

Built in 1855, the Italianate country house known as Cedar Hill was the last home of abolitionist Frederick Douglass. Decorative arts, libraries and family mementoes provide an intimate look at his life and work.

Slave America's famous abolitionist was born into slavery in Maryland around 1818 and separated from his mother at birth. When Douglass was 12, his master's wife illegally taught him to read. He escaped to Maryland when he was 20, becoming active in the Massachusetts anti-slavery movement. He wrote an autobiography in 1845, which became so popular that he fled to Europe out of fear that his former master would find out and he would be recaptured. There, British friends bought him his freedom, and he lectured widely on anti-slavery topics. When he moved into Cedar Hill, he became the first black resident of Anacostia, breaking the prohibition against "Irish, Negro, mulatto or persons of African blood."

Viewpoint Cedar Hill, now the Frederick Douglass National Historic Site, occupies the highest point in Anacostia, with views of the Anacostia River and the capital. At his desk in the library, Douglass wrote his autobiography *The Life and Times of Frederick Douglass*. The National Park Service, which manages the site, maintains a visitor center and a bookstore specializing in African-American titles.

More to See

ANACOSTIA COMMUNITY MUSEUM

anacostia.si.edu

This museum displays documents that interpret the impact of historical and modern social issues on urban communities.

➕ See map ▷ 97   ✉ 1901 Fort Place SE   ☎ 202/633-4820   🕐 Daily 10–5   🚇 Anacostia, then bus W2. D.C. Circulator Union Station–Congress Heights route to Anacostia metro, then bus W2   💲 Free

NATIONAL ARBORETUM

usna.usda.gov

The Arboretum's many acres invite driving, biking and hiking. See the National Herb Garden, National Bonsai Collection and Azalea Walk.

➕ See map ▷ 97   ✉ 3501 New York Avenue NE   ☎ 202/245-2726   🕐 Daily 8–5. Weekend tram tours Apr–Oct   🚇 Stadium-Armory, then bus B2   💲 Free

OLD TOWN, ALEXANDRIA

visitalexandria.com

A well-preserved colonial port town, Old Town's cobblestone streets are packed with early-American homes and taverns. A popular picnic spot.

➕ See map ▷ 96   ✉ Old Town, Alexandria, VA   🚇 King Street–Old Town

SHRINE OF THE IMMACULATE CONCEPTION

nationalshrine.org

Dedicated to the Virgin Mary, and the largest church in North America, this Catholic basilica is renowned for its mosaics.

➕ See map ▷ 97   ✉ 400 Michigan Avenue NE   ☎ 202/526-8300   🕐 Apr–Oct daily 7–7; Nov–Mar 7–6. Hourly tours Mon–Sat 9–11, 1–3, Sun 1.30–3.30   💲 Free   🚇 Brookland CUA

THEODORE ROOSEVELT ISLAND

nps.gov/this

This island in the Potomac River has miles of walking trails through diverse terrain. A tall bronze statue of Roosevelt can be found in the center of the island.

➕ C5   ☎ 703/289-2500   🕐 Daily 6am–10pm   🚗 Car access from northbound lane of George Washington Memorial Parkway

Hydrangeas in the National Arboretum

The Theodore Roosevelt Monument on Theodore Roosevelt Island

Excursions

FREDERICKSBURG

The 40-block National Historic District in this charming Virginia town comprises the house George Washington (1732–99) bought for his mother, a 1752 plantation, the law offices of President James Monroe (1758–1831), an early apothecary shop owned by Hugh Mercer and the Georgian Chatham Manor, which overlooks the Rappahannock River.

Two Civil War battles were waged in and around town. You can now visit the battlefields and stroll through the nearby wilderness parks. Antiques and rare-book stores and art galleries line the streets. Start at the well-marked visitor center, which dispenses maps and advice.

THE BASICS

visitfred.com
Distance: 50 miles (80km)
Journey Time: 1–2 hours
🚩 706 Caroline Street
☎ 540/373-1776
🕐 Daily 9–5, extended summer hours
🚆 Amtrak from Union Station
🚗 South on I-95 to exit 133A and follow signs to visitor center

GEORGE WASHINGTON'S MOUNT VERNON

This ancestral Virginia estate is the nation's second-most visited historic house after the White House. Washington worked this vast plantation's 8,000 acres (3,239ha) before he took control of the Continental Army and returned here for good after his presidency.

Washington supervised the expansion of the main house, most notably the addition of the back porch with a view over the Potomac. The mansion is built of yellow pine, then painted multiple times with sand in order to resemble stone. The ornate interior is furnished with fine arts and memorabilia, and history interpreters provide more information. The outbuildings re-create the spaces of a self-sufficient, 18th-century farm, including the smokehouse and laundry, outside kitchen and slave quarters. Don't miss the view of George and Martha Washington's tomb, and allow time to explore the formal garden and follow the forest trail. The Ladies Association was founded in 1853 to preserve the estate.

THE BASICS

mountvernon.org
Distance: 15 miles (24km)
Journey Time: 40 minutes
☎ 703/780-2000
🕐 Apr–Oct daily 9–5; Nov–Mar 9–4
🚆 Huntington Station, then Fairfax Connector bus
🚗 Take 14th Street Bridge (toward National Airport), then south on George Washington Memorial Parkway
🚢 *Spirit of Mount Vernon* from Pier 4, 6th and Water streets SW (☎ 866/302-2469) Mar–Oct and Mon holidays 💲 Expensive

Shopping

FASHION CENTRE

Macy's and Nordstrom anchor the 170 stores in this Pentagon City mall.

🔲 Off map at C9 ▨ 1100 S Hayes Street at Army-Navy Drive and I-395 S ☎ 703/415-2400 🕔 Mon–Sat 10–9.30, Sun 11–6 🚇 Pentagon City

FRIENDSHIP HEIGHTS

These three shopping malls cater to any need. The upscale Mazza Gallerie and the Chevy Chase Pavilion across the street contain a range of shops including Neiman Marcus at Mazza. The über-chic Collection at Chevy Chase has Saks and Tiffany.

🔲 Off map at A1 ▨ Wisconsin Avenue at Western Avenue 🕔 Mazza Gallerie: Mon–Fri 10–8, Sat 10–7, Sun 12–6. Chevy Chase Pavilion: Mon–Sat 10–8, Sun 11–6. Collection at Chevy Chase: hours vary 🚇 Friendship Heights

HOUSE OF MUSICAL TRADITIONS

hmtrad.com

Musical instruments from lap dulcimers to bagpipes are sold at this well-known store, established in 1972.

🔲 Off map at J1 ▨ 7010 Westmoreland Avenue, Takoma Park, MD ☎ 301/270-9090 🕔 Tue–Sat 11–7, Sun–Mon 11–5 🚇 Takoma

POTOMAC MILLS MALL

This is one of Virginia's most popular retail destinations. Shoppers will enjoy Banana Republic and Polo at a discount.

🔲 Off map at A9 ▨ 2700 Potomac Mills Circle, Woodbridge, VA ☎ 703/496-9330 🕔 Mon–Sat 10–9, Sun 11–6 🚇 Franconia-Springfield 🚗 Via I-95 S

TANGER OUTLETS

tangeroutlet.com/nationalharbor.com

Shop at over 85 brands then take in the other sites at the massive National Harbor development.

🔲 Off map at H9 ▨ 6800 Oxon Hill Road, National Harbor, MD ☎ 301/567-3880 🕔 Mon–Sat 9–9, Sun 10–7 🚗 5.5 miles (9km) via I295

TORPEDO FACTORY ART CENTER

torpedofactory.org

Come here for pottery, paintings, jewelry, stained glass and other items by local artists, who work in the studios of this former U.S. Naval torpedo station.

🔲 Off map at F9 ▨ 105 N Union Street, Alexandria, VA ☎ 703/746 4576 🕔 Daily 10–6, Thu till 9pm 🚇 King Street, then free trolley Sun–Wed 10.30–10.30, Thu–Sat 10.30am–midnight

TYSONS CORNER CENTER

tysonscornercenter.com

Tysons Corner Center claims Nordstrom, Bloomingdale's and an AMC theater. Tysons Galleria, across the highway, is a little more upscale, with Saks Fifth Avenue and Chanel.

🔲 Off map at A2 ▨ 1961 Chain Bridge Road, Tysons Corner, VA ☎ 703/893 9400 🕔 Center: Mon–Sat 10–9.30, Sun 11–7. Galleria: Mon–Sat 10–9, Sun 12–6 🚇 Tysons Corner 🚗 I–66 west to Route 7 west, then follow signs

---

ROYAL TREATMENT

Political staffers don't shirk from putting in time at work, but they also like to be pampered. Want to see partisans reeling from a recent loss or reveling in a clear victory? Head to: Spa by Ivanka Trump (☎ 202/868-5180), Blue Mercury (▷ 90), Grooming Lounge (▷ 29) or Roche Salon (☎ 202/775-0775). Some of the top-end hotels, like the Mandarin Oriental (▷ 112), the Ritz-Carlton (▷ 112) and the Willard (▷ 112), have spas offering you the ultimate in superb treatments.

Entertainment and Nightlife

ARENA STAGE

arenastage.org

This company presents dynamically staged and superbly acted theater.

H8 ✉ 1101 6th Street SW ☎ 202/554-9066 🚇 Waterfront

BIRCHMERE

birchmere.com

One of America's top spots to catch the best bluegrass and folk acts around.

Off map at D9 ✉ 3701 Mount Vernon Avenue, Alexandria, VA ☎ 703/549-7500 🕐 Check website for shows 🚇 Pentagon City, then taxi

CONTINENTAL

continentalpoollounge.com

This billiards hall is adorned with bright, retro decor and several cozy lounges, perfect for relaxing between games.

B5 ✉ 1911 North Fort Myer Drive, Arlington, VA ☎ 703/465-7675 🕐 Mon–Fri 11.30am–2am, Sat–Sun 6pm–?am 🚇 Rosslyn

THE FILLMORE

fillmoresilverspring.com

This opulent venue dishes up regular well-known national acts. Be prepared to stand.

Off map at H1 ✉ 8656 Colesville Road, Silver Spring, MD ☎ 301/960-9999 🕐 Box office Mon–Fri 12–6, Sat 11–4 🚇 Silver Spring

POLITICAL PUNCHLINES

The Constituents, at theaters around DC, take aim at both sides of the political divide. As do Capitol Steps (☎ 703/683-8330), former and current Hill staffers. Washington Improv Theater (WIT) (☎ 202/315-1318) and ComedySportz (☎ 202/296-7008) tend toward more traditional improv, while D.C. Improv (☎ 202/296-7008) delivers well-known stand-up acts.

ROCK AND ROLL HOTEL

rockandrollhoteldc.com

A popular live-music venue that plays host to solid indie bands.

M5 ✉ 1353 H Street NE ☎ 202/388-7625 🕐 Check website for shows: 6pm–late on days open for shows 🚇 Union Station, then 15-block walk

ROUND HOUSE THEATRE

roundhousetheatre.org

The Round House Theatre presents an eclectic program of plays.

Off map at A1 ✉ 4545 East-West Highway, Bethesda, MD ☎ 240/644-1100 🚇 Bethesda

SIGNATURE THEATRE

sigtheatre.org

This theater is renowned for its sharply produced musicals, especially those of Steven Sondheim.

Off map at A9 ✉ 4200 Campbell Avenue, Arlington, VA ☎ 703/820-9771 🕐 Box office Mon–Fri 10–6, Sat–Sun 12–6 🚇 Pentagon City, then taxi

STRATHMORE

strathmore.org

This music venue has great acoustics. It hosts the Baltimore Symphony Orchestra and the National Philharmonic.

Off map at A1 ✉ 5301 Tuckerman Lane, North Bethesda, MD ☎ 301/581-5100 🚇 Grovesnor–Strathmore

WOLF TRAP

wolftrap.org

This popular venue draws top music acts, dance and musical theater to its outdoor amphitheater. When it's cold, shows are transferred to the Barns at Wolf Trap.

Off map at A1 ✉ Trap Road, Vienna, VA ☎ 703/255-1900 🚇 West Falls Church, then Wolf Trap express bus (in summer only)

Where to Eat

ETHIOPIC ($$)
ethiopicrestaurant.com
Doro wat (chicken stew), tangy *injera* (bread) and colorful vegetables star at this light-filled restaurant that serves authentic Ethiopian dishes.
➕ M5 ✉ 401 H Street NE ☎ 202/675-2066
🕐 Tue–Thu 5–10, Fri–Sun 12–10 🚇 Union Station, then taxi or bus X2

GREEN PIG BISTRO ($)
greenpigbistro.com
Hearty classic French cooking with an American twist. Reservations not allowed for lunch.
➕ Off map at A7 ✉ 1025 N Fillmore, Arlington ☎ 703/888-1920 🕐 Mon–Fri 11–2, Sun–Tue 5.30–9.30, Wed–Sat 5.30–10, brunch Sat–Sun 10.30–12.30 🚇 Clarendon Station, then walk

GUARDADO'S ($$)
guardados.com
Flavorful dishes from Spain and Latin America including tapas. A must-try is the shrimp sautéed with garlic.
➕ Off map at B1 ✉ 4918 Del Ray Avenue, Bethesda ☎ 301/986-4920 🕐 Tue–Thu 12–9, Fri–Sat 12–10, Sun 5–9 🚇 Bethesda

KALIWA ($$)
kaliwadc.com
Cathal Armstrong's funky space offers a menu inspired by the Philippines, Korea, and Thailand.
➕ Off map at G9 ✉ 751 Wharf Street SW ☎ 202/516-4739 🕐 Lunch and dinner daily from 11.30am 🚇 Waterfront-SEU, then 10-min walk

THE MAJESTIC ($–$$)
themajesticva.com
This bistro restaurant in an historic Old Town building serves seasonal contemporary American cuisine.
➕ Off map at D5 ✉ 911 King Street, Old Town, Alexandria ☎ 703/837-9117 🕐 Mon–Thu 11.30am–midnight, Fri 11.30am–1am, Sat 10am–1am, Sun 10am–midnight 🚇 King Street then Old Town trolleybus

PHO 75 ($)
Pho, a Vietnamese noodle dish often eaten at breakfast in Vietnam, is served here in nearly 20 varieties—all of them tasty. Forks are provided if you're not adept with chopsticks.
➕ A6 ✉ 1721 Wilson Boulevard, Arlington, VA ☎ 703/525-7355 🕐 Daily 9–9 🚇 Rosslyn, then 10-min walk

SUSHIKO ($$)
sushikorestaurants.com
Chefs and brothers Piter Tjan and Handry Tjan serve top-notch sushi. Order the tasting menu and rest assured you'll be wowed by their inventive fare.
➕ Off map at B1 ✉ 5455 Wisconsin Avenue, Chevy Chase ☎ 301/961-1644 🕐 Mon–Fri 12–3, 5.30–10, Sat–Sun 12–3, 5.30–10.30 🚇 Friendship Heights

TOKI UNDERGROUND ($$)
tokiunderground.com
Many diners have developed a love affair with ramen after a visit to this Taiwanese and Japanese hot spot. And the entrance is, in fact, at street level.
➕ M5 ✉ 1234 H Street NE ☎ 202/388-3086 🕐 Mon–Sat 11.30–2.30, Mon–Thu 5–10, Fri–Sat 5–midnight 🚇 Union Station, then taxi or bus X2

Where to Stay

With options ranging from the luxurious to simple budget hotels, Washington has a place to stay for everyone.

Introduction **108**

Budget Hotels **109**

Mid-Range Hotels **110**

Luxury Hotels **112**

Introduction

Washington's hotels suit everyone, from those in town for all the free museums to deep-pocket lobbyists, and from culture lovers to seekers of star chefs.

Diplomats at Breakfast
The high-end and business-class hotels tend to be near the halls of power, whether at the White House or on Capitol Hill. Downtown and Georgetown play host to a fair share of luxury properties as well. There's a good chance that if you stay in one of the pricier places, you'll run into diplomats at breakfast and brush shoulders with heads of state (or their security guards) in the elevator, or notice a Hollywood celebrity sitting in the bar, in town for a film shoot.

A Slower Pace
D.C.'s smaller hotels and guesthouses are in the leafier areas of northwest D.C. Guests in these areas will enjoy a slightly slower pace and smaller crowds, and it's only a short hop to the Mall and Hill.

Off Season? Not in D.C.
Summers bring tourists and winters bring policy makers and lobbyists. In fact, when Congress is in session, it's often more expensive to get a room during the week than on the weekend. Your best bet is to head for the suburbs, which are convenient for Metro stops.

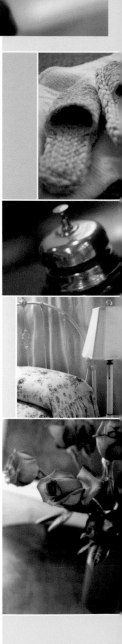

WHERE THE PRESIDENTS LIVE

In the White House, correct? Not when it's being renovated. George Washington lived in New York and Philadelphia before the Capitol moved to D.C. James Madison lived in the Octagon House (18th Street NW and New York Avenue) after the British burned the White House to the ground. Calvin Coolidge hosted Charles Lindbergh at the Patterson House (15 Dupont Circle) while the White House was being renovated. Harry S. Truman moved out for renovations also—to the nearby Blair House at 1651 Pennsylvania Avenue, where two Puerto Rican nationalists tried to assassinate him.

Budget Hotels

Mall and many of the city's museums are just a few blocks away.
➕ G6 ✉ 436 11th Street NW ☎ 202/628-8140 🚇 Metro Center

ADAMS INN

adamsinn.com

This clean, simple yet cozy Victorian B&B encompasses three houses on a quiet street near Adams Morgan.
➕ F1 ✉ 1746 Lanier Place NW ☎ 202/745-3600 🚇 Woodley Park–Zoo, then 10-min walk

AMERICANA HOTEL

americanahotel.com

Step back in time at this family-owned hotel—the style is a throwback to the 1960s when it first opened.
➕ Off map at C9 ✉ 1400 Richmond Highway, Arlington, VA ☎ 703/979-3772 🚇 Pentagon City, Crystal City

EMBASSY ROW HOTEL

embassyrowhotel.com

You'll find this vibrant, stylish property in cosmopolitan Dupont Circle. It's well-known for its rooftop bar and pool.
➕ E3 ✉ 2015 Massachusetts Avenue NW ☎ 202/265-1600 🚇 Dupont Circle

GEORGETOWN INN

georgetowninn.com

Opened during the Kennedy presidency, this elegant hotel is very much at home amid the Federal-era architecture of the neighborhood.
➕ C4 ✉ 1310 Wisconsin Avenue NW ☎ 202/333-8900 🚇 Foggy Bottom, then 15-min walk

HOTEL HARRINGTON

hotel-harrington.com

This is your basic, no-frills hotel with the addition of two restaurants and a pub. The hotel is also in a great location—the

HOTEL TABARD INN

tabardinn.com

This charming old inn with plush rooms also sports a cozy lounge with a fireplace and a top-notch restaurant.
➕ F4 ✉ 1739 N Street NW ☎ 202/785-1277 🚇 Dupont Circle

KALORAMA GUEST HOUSE

kaloramaguesthouse.com

This charming Victorian B&B is filled with 19th-century furnishings and books in every room.
➕ E2 ✉ 2700 Cathedral Avenue NW ☎ 202/588-8188 🚇 Woodley Park–Zoo

WINDSOR PARK HOTEL

windsorparkhotel.com

In a leafy suburb, this pleasant hotel is just a short walk from Rock Creek Park. A free continental breakfast is included.
➕ E2 ✉ 2116 Kalorama Road NW ☎ 202/483-7700 🚇 Dupont Circle

WOODLEY PARK GUEST HOUSE

dcinns.com

This intimate bed-and-breakfast near the zoo has individualized rooms filled with antiques. Young children are not allowed.
➕ D1 ✉ 2647 Woodley Road NW ☎ 202/667-0218 🚇 Woodley Park–Zoo

BED-AND-BREAKFAST

To find reasonably priced accommodations in small guesthouses and private homes, contact Bed & Breakfast Accommodations (✉ 1339 14th Street NW, Washington D.C., 20005 ☎ 202/328-3510, bedandbreakfastdc.com).

Mid-Range Hotels

PRICES
Expect to pay between $190 and $325 per night for a double room in a mid-range hotel.

AKWAABA DC

akwaaba.com

A literary-themed luxurious bed-and-breakfast owned by the former editor of *Essence*, Akwaaba sits in a well-located town house.

➕ F3 ✉ 1708 16th Street NW ☎ 866/466-3855 Ⓜ Dupont Circle

BEACON HOTEL

beaconhotelwdc.com

With a popular bar and grill, this lively hotel has well-sized, light-filled rooms arguably aimed more at the business traveler. The larger suites come with kitchenettes.

➕ F4 ✉ 1615 Rhode Island Avenue NW ☎ 202/296-2100 Ⓜ Dupont Circle

CAPITOL HILL HOTEL

capitolhillhotel-dc.com

Close to the Library of Congress and the Capitol, this family- and pet-friendly all-suites hotel encompasses two smart buildings. Breakfast is included and the rooms have a chic modern look.

➕ K7 ✉ 200 C Street SE ☎ 202/543-6000 Ⓜ Capitol South

EMBASSY CIRCLE GUEST HOUSE

dcinns.com/dupont-circle-bed-and-breakfast

The rooms in this immaculately restored Georgian Revival mansion feel airy and modern yet rooted in the classic, with thick Persian rugs in every room. Breakfast is included but note that there are no TVs or radios in this guesthouse.

➕ E3 ✉ 2224 R Street NW ☎ 202/232-7744 Ⓜ Dupont Circle

THE FAIRFAX AT EMBASSY ROW

fairfaxwashingtondc.com

On one of Washington's loveliest streets, the classically appointed Fairfax offers an elegant respite from the bustle of nearby Dupont Circle.

➕ E3 ✉ 2100 Massachusetts Avenue NW ☎ 202/293-2100 Ⓜ Dupont Circle

THE GRAHAM GEORGETOWN

thegrahamgeorgetown.com

A conservative facade contrasts with the contemporary glamor found inside this property sited on a charming side street. The seasonal rooftop bar offers spectacular views.

➕ D4 ✉ 1075 Thomas Jefferson Street NW ☎ 202/337-0900 Ⓜ Foggy Bottom, then 10-min walk

HENLEY PARK HOTEL

henleypark.com

Built in 1918 (as apartments), this Tudor-style hotel has charming architectural details such as gargoyles. The hotel serves formal tea each afternoon. Some rooms are a little tired.

➕ H5 ✉ 926 Massachusetts Avenue NW ☎ 202/638-5200 Ⓜ Mount Vernon Square, Metro Center

HOTEL MONACO

monaco-dc.com

Built in 1839 by the designer of the Washington Monument, the Monaco has very striking, modern rooms with vaulted ceilings around a landscaped courtyard.

➕ H5 ✉ 700 F Street NW ☎ 202/628-7177 Ⓜ Gallery Place–Chinatown

HOTEL PALOMAR

hotelpalomar-dc.com

This arts-themed Kimpton hotel with stylish and fun rooms hosts a wine-tasting every evening. The many amenities include an outdoor pool, and pets can stay at no extra charge.

➕ E4 ✉ 2121 P Street NW ☎ 202/448-1800 🚇 Dupont Circle

HOTEL ROUGE
rougehotel.com

Decked out in rich reds and contrasting pale colors, Rouge, another Kimpton hotel, appeals to style-savvy visitors who value its location between the White House and Dupont Circle.

➕ F4 ✉ 1315 16th Street NW ☎ 202/232-8000 🚇 Dupont Circle

LIAISON CAPITOL HILL
liaisondc.com

The Liaison's prime location makes it ideal for visits to many of the major attractions. It has the largest rooftop pool and bar in the city.

➕ J6 ✉ 415 New Jersey Avenue NW ☎ 202/638 1616 🚇 Union Station

MARRIOTT WARDMAN PARK
marriott.com/WASDT

This large hotel with conference facilities on 16 acres (6.5ha) rises above the Woodley Park Metro stop and has a good view of Rock Creek Park.

➕ D1 ✉ 2660 Woodley Road NW ☎ 202/328-2000 🚇 Woodley Park–Zoo

MORRISON-CLARK INN HOTEL
morrisonclark.com

Created by merging two 1864 town houses, this gracious inn has modern touches in all its rooms and spaces.

➕ G4 ✉ 1011 L Street NW ☎ 202/898-1200 🚇 Mount Vernon Square, Metro Center

THE NORMANDY HOTEL
thenormandydc.com

This European-style hotel, on a quiet embassy-lined street, is popular among diplomats. There's a wine-and-cheese reception in the evening and guests are given complimentary access to gym passes for a local sports club.

➕ E2 ✉ 2118 Wyoming Avenue NW ☎ 202/483-1350 🚇 Dupont Circle

THE PHOENIX PARK HOTEL
phoenixparkhotel.com

Bask in the aura and elegance of an 18th-century Irish estate steps away from the U.S. Capitol. The Phoenix Park Hotel has served statesmen, tourists and diplomats since 1922.

➕ J5 ✉ 520 N Capitol Street NW ☎ 202/638-6900 🚇 Union Station

SWANN HOUSE
swannhouse.com

Converted from an 1883 Dupont Circle mansion, this bed-and-breakfast wows with feather beds, chandeliers and original molding.

➕ F3 ✉ 1808 New Hampshire Avenue NW ☎ 202/265-4414 🚇 Dupont Circle

TOPAZ HOTEL
topazhotel.com

Colorful Moroccan and Le Cirque influences complement the airy feel to this wellness-themed hotel with in-room yoga mats.

➕ F4 ✉ 1733 N Street NW ☎ 202/393-3000 🚇 Dupont Circle

WASHINGTON PLAZA
washingtonplazahotel.com

This hotel was designed by Miami architect Morris Lapidus in the 1960s. While the rooms are simple and functional, aimed more at the business traveler, the outdoor pool area gives this hotel a resort-like feel.

➕ G4 ✉ 10 Thomas Circle NW ☎ 202/842-1300 🚇 McPherson Square

Luxury Hotels

PRICES

Expect to pay more than $325 per night for a double room in a luxury hotel.

FOUR SEASONS HOTEL

fourseasons.com/washington

A gathering place for Washington's elite, this hotel features custom-made furniture and original artwork.
➕ D4 ✉ 2800 Pennsylvania Avenue NW
☎ 202/342-0444 🚇 Foggy Bottom

HAY-ADAMS HOTEL

hayadams.com

Looking like a mansion on the outside and an English country house within, this hotel has a great White House view—ask for a room on the south side.
➕ F5 ✉ 800 16th Street NW ☎ 202/638-6600 🚇 McPherson Square

THE JEFFERSON

jeffersondc.com

Antiques and presidential paraphernalia can be found inside this Beaux Arts building, alongside modern amenities such as the huge glass bar in the center of the hotel's elegant lounge.
➕ F5 ✉ 1200 16th Street NW ☎ 202/448-2300 🚇 McPherson Square

MANDARIN ORIENTAL

mandarinoriental.com/washington

This large hotel, with a superb spa, features rooms with an Asian flare.

BOOKING AGENCY

For help finding hotels (both chain and boutique style), bed-and-breakfasts and campgrounds in the D.C. area, as well as events and activities, check out Destination D.C.'s website: washington.org or call toll-free on 800/422-8644.

Restaurants, Amity & Commerce (▷ 52) and Empress Lounge, are popular.
➕ H7 ✉ 1330 Maryland Avenue SW
☎ 202/554-8588 🚇 Smithsonian

THE MAYFLOWER

themayflowerhotel.com

The lobby of this grand hotel glistens with gilded trim. The rooms have hosted many presidents, celebrities and royalty.
➕ F4 ✉ 1127 Connecticut Avenue NW
☎ 202/347-3000 🚇 Farragut North

RITZ-CARLTON, GEORGETOWN

ritzcarlton.com

In spite of the fact this used to be an industrial building, this sleek hotel is luxurious and cozy. Pets are welcome.
➕ C4 ✉ 3100 South Street NW ☎ 202/912-4100 🚇 Foggy Bottom, then 15-min walk

ROSEWOOD WASHINGTON DC

rosewoodhotels.com

This Georgetown hotel is beside the C&O canal, and combines classic design with the latest technology. The rooftop bar is a hot spot when it's fine.
➕ D4 ✉ 1050 31st Street NW ☎ 202/617-2400 🚇 Foggy Bottom, then 15-min walk

SOFITEL, LAFAYETTE SQUARE

sofitel-washington-dc.com

Sophisticated style and impeccable service are combined at this French influenced hotel with high-quality rooms.
➕ G5 ✉ 806 15th Street NW ☎ 202/730-8800 🚇 McPherson Square

WILLARD INTERCONTINENTAL

washington.intercontinental.com

Heads of state have stayed at the Willard Intercontinental since 1853. The Round Robin Bar is justly famous.
➕ G5 ✉ 1401 Pennsylvania Avenue NW
☎ 800/424-6835 🚇 Metro Center

Need to Know

This section takes you through all the practical aspects of your trip to make it run more smoothly.

Planning Ahead   **114**

Getting There   **116**

Getting Around   **118**

Essential Facts   **120**

Timeline   **124**

Planning Ahead

When to Go

There is no bad time to visit Washington. Spring is busiest, when the city's cherry trees are in blossom. October and November bring brilliant foliage. Summer, although crowded and sweltering, sees a chockablock calendar of special events, many of which are free.

AVERAGE DAILY MAXIMUM TEMPERATURES

JAN	FEB	MAR	APR	MAY	JUN	JUL	AUG	SEP	OCT	NOV	DEC
43°F	47°F	56°F	67°F	74°F	84°F	89°F	87°F	80°F	68°F	58°F	47°F
6°C	8°C	13°C	19°C	23°C	29°C	31°C	30°C	26°C	20°C	14°C	8°C

Spring (mid-March to May) is extremely pleasant, with flowers and trees in bloom throughout the city.

Summer (June to early September) is hot and humid, with temperatures sometimes reaching 95°F (35°C) or more.

Fall (mid-September to November) is comfortable, and sometimes bracing.

Winter (December to mid-March) varies from year to year: It can be extremely cold or surprisingly warm. The occasional snowfall shuts the city down.

WHAT'S ON

January *Antiques Show* (washingtonwintershow.com).
Martin Luther King, Jr. Birthday Observations.
Restaurant Week (ramw.org/restaurantweek).
February *Presidents' Day. Chinese New Year's Parade* (sometimes takes place in January).
March *St. Patrick's Day Festival* (shamrockfest.com).
Environmental Film Festival (dceff.org).
April *National Cherry Blossom Festival*

(nationalcherry blossomfestival.org).
White House Spring Garden Tour (whitehouse.gov).
Filmfest DC (filmfestdc.org).
May *Passport DC* (culturaltourismdc.org).
Memorial Day Concert.
June *Capital Pride Festival* (capitalpride.org).
Military Band Summer Concert Series (aoc.gov).
June/July *Smithsonian Folklife Festival* (festival.si.edu).
July *Independence Day* (Jul 4, nps.gov).
Capital Fringe Festival

(capitalfringe.org).
September *National Symphony Orchestra Labor Day Concert* (kennedy-center.org).
October *Marine Corps Marathon* (marinemarathon.com).
Taste of DC Festival (thetasteofdc.org).
November *Veterans' Day.*
December *National Christmas Tree Lighting* (thenationaltree.org).
You can find information about events in the area on the travel site washington.org.

Washington Online

si.edu
The Smithsonian Institution site features a directory of its 18 museums, schedules of events and exhibitions, information about publications and a link to the gift shop.

washington.org
This site is presented by the Washington, D.C. Convention and Tourism board. You can make hotel reservations, gather information about the different neighborhoods and find out about annual events.

culturaltourismdc.org
The website of this nonprofit coalition of D.C. cultural and neighborhood organizations has comprehensive and easy-to-navigate listings of D.C. districts, walks, events and attractions that you might not be able to find elsewhere.

opentable.com
Allows diners to check availability and make reservations at most Washington restaurants.

washingtonpost.com
The newspaper's site features a going out guide, airport status reports, calendar of events and reviews of nightlife and restaurants.

washingtoncitypaper.com
The site of this alternative weekly carries the newspaper's superb arts and restaurant coverage, with reviews from the paper's critics and visitors to the site.

senate.gov and house.gov
Congress website including information on upcoming votes, history and how to visit.

goDCgo.com
This online hub of the District Department of Transportation (DDOT) provides everything you need to know about traveling by public transportation in D.C.

fodors.com
A complete travel-planning site. You can research prices and weather; book air tickets, cars and rooms; ask questions (and get answers) from fellow travelers; and find links to other sites.

wmata.com
The Washington Metropolitan Area Transit Authority site features comprehensive maps of the Metro and bus systems, plus information on delays and vacation schedules.

Getting There

BUS TRAVEL

Several bus companies—some with free WiFi—pick up passengers throughout Washington and offer inexpensive rides to New York. Try bestbus.com or boltbus.com.

TRAIN TRAVEL

Amtrak (amtrak.com) trains leave on tracks stretching out the back of Union Station. The service to New York takes 3–4 hours; it's almost 8 hours to Boston. The high-speed Acela cuts journeys down to less than 3 hours and 6.5 hours respectively. Two less-expensive commuter lines service the Virginia and Maryland suburbs on weekdays.

VISAS FOR THE U.S.

Visitors traveling on a full British passport are required to obtain an electronic authorization to travel. Go to the official U.S. government website esta.cbp.dhs.gov to apply and pay the fee by credit card.

AIRPORTS

D.C. is 1 hour 15 minutes from New York, 5 hours 40 minutes from Los Angeles and 6 hours 45 minutes from London. The major airports include Reagan National Airport, Dulles International Airport and Baltimore-Washington International Thurgood Marshall Airport (BWI).

FROM REAGAN NATIONAL AIRPORT

Reagan National Airport (tel 703/417-8000, flyreagan.com) is in Virginia, 4 miles (6.4km) south of Downtown and the closest to central Washington. A taxi to Downtown takes about 20 minutes and costs around $15–$25. SuperShuttle (tel 800/258-3826, supershuttle.com) offers airport-to-door service for $19 per person 24 hours a day. The blue and yellow Metro lines run from the airport to Downtown, with stations next to terminals B and C (Mon–Thu 5am–11.30pm, Fri 5am–1am, Sat 7am–1am, Sun 7am–11pm). SmarTrip fare cards can be bought from machines on level 2 near the pedestrian bridges linking the two terminals and can be loaded or reloaded with any amount you choose. For Metro information call 202/637-7000.

RMA (tel 888/727 1636; rmalimo.com) will arrange for a vehicle to meet you at the airport; costs from $100, plus a 20 percent gratuity.

FROM DULLES INTERNATIONAL AIRPORT

Dulles International Airport (tel 703/572-2700, flydulles.com) is 26 miles (42km) west of

Washington. A taxi to the city takes around 40 minutes and costs around $70–$80. The Silver Line Express Bus (tel 703/572-7661) goes from the airport to the Wiehle–Reston East Metro. Buses leave the airport every 15–20 minutes Mon–Fri 6am–10.40pm, Sat 7.45am–10.40pm, Sun 7.45am–9.40pm. The 15-minute trip costs $5 ($10 round-trip). SuperShuttle (tel 800/258-3826) costs $33 per person, plus $10 for each additional person. RMA (tel 888/727-1636) costs around $130 for a sedan, plus a 20 percent gratuity.

FROM BWI AIRPORT

Baltimore-Washington International Thurgood Marshall Airport, (tel 410/859 7111, bwiairport.com), is in Maryland, 30 miles (48km) northeast of Washington. A taxi from the airport takes around 45 minutes and costs $90. SuperShuttle (tel 800/258-3826) costs $37, plus $12 for each additional person. Free shuttle buses run between airline terminals and the train station. Amtrak (tel 800/872-7245, amtrak.com) and MARC (tel 866/743-3682, mta.maryland.gov) trains run between the airport and Union Station. The 40-minute ride costs $15–$45 (depending on day and time) on Amtrak and $9 on MARC. With RMA you'll pay $150 for a sedan, plus a 20 percent gratuity.

INSURANCE

Check your policy and buy any necessary supplements. It is vital that travel insurance covers medical expenses, in addition to accident, trip cancellation, baggage loss and theft. Also make sure the policy covers any continuing treatment for a more chronic condition.

ENTRY REQUIREMENTS

For the latest passport and visa information, look up the embassy website at uk.usembassy.gov. The authorities are now subjecting more people to even more security checks. To avoid problems allow plenty of time for clearing security, and be sure to check the latest advice. See also the panel opposite.

AIRLINES

Major air carriers serving the three airports (Reagan National Airport, Dulles International Airport and Baltimore-Washington International Airport) include:

Air Canada	☎ 888/247-2262
Air France	☎ 800/237-2747
American Airlines	☎ 800/433-7300
British Airways	☎ 800/247-9297
Delta	☎ 800/221-1212
Emirates	☎ 800/777-3999
Frontier Airlines	☎ 801/401-9000
Icelandair	☎ 800/223-5500
KLM Royal Dutch	☎ 866/434-0320
Lufthansa	☎ 800/645-3880
Saudi Arabian Airlines	☎ 800/472-8342
Scandinavian Airlines	☎ 800/221-2350
United	☎ 800/864-8331
Virgin Atlantic	☎ 800/862-8621

For less expensive flights contact:
Southwest Airlines ☎ 800/435-9792
Spirit Airlines ☎ 801/401-2222 or
JetBlue Airways ☎ 800/538-2583

Getting Around

NEED TO KNOW   GETTING AROUND

CAPITAL BIKESHARE

The region's bike-sharing service has more than 4,300 bicycles available at more than 500 stations in the area.

● Sign up online (capital bikeshare.com) and select from 30-minute rides ($2) to three-day passes ($17) or longer memberships.

● Take a bike from any Bikeshare station. Users must provide their own bike helmet.

● Return the bike to any Bikeshare station. Bikeshare is available year round.

PUBLIC TRANSPORTATION

● The subway (Metro) and bus (Metrobus) systems are run by the Washington Metropolitan Area Transit Authority (WMATA).

● Maps of the Metro system and some bus schedules are available in all Metro stations or at WMATA headquarters (600 5th Street NW).

● For general information, call 202/637-7000, open Mon–Fri 7am–8pm, Sat–Sun 8am–6.30pm, wmata.com.

● The WMATA website is updated throughout the day showing problems on individual routes.

● For Lost and Found, call 202/962-1195; for Transit Police call 202/962-2121.

BUSES

● Bus signs are blue, red and white.

● The bus system covers a much wider area than the Metro.

● The fare within the city is $2.

● Free bus-to-bus transfers are available when using a SmarTrip card and are good for about 2 hours at designated Metrobus transfer points.

● If you use cash, make sure you have the exact change as bus drivers don't carry money.

● A 7-day regional SmarTrip bus pass costs $15.

METRO

● The city's subway system, the Metro, is one of the cleanest and safest in the country. You need a farecard, called a SmarTrip card, loaded with money to pay the fare and to enter and exit the train area. Farecard machines, located in the stations, take coins and $1, $5, $10 and $20 bills. The most change the machine will give you is about $10, so don't use a large bill if you are buying a low-value card.

● Metro stations are marked by tall brown pillars with a large, white "M" at the top. A colored stripe under the "M" indicates the line or lines that are serviced by the station.

● Trains run every few minutes on Mon–Thu 5am–11.30pm, Fri 5am–1am, Sat 7am–1am, Sun 7am–11.30pm.

● The basic peak fare ($2.25) increases with

the length of your trip. It is cheaper at off-peak times. Maps in stations tell you both the rush-hour fare and regular fare to any destination station. A one-day pass is $13.

● Tap the SmarTrip card on the fare gate on entry and exit.

D.C. CIRCULATOR

● An alternative to the Metro, the red buses of the D.C. Circulator run every 10 minutes on five routes connecting places of interest and are free of charge. Routes: Dupont Circle–Georgetown–Rosslyn; Georgetown–Union Station; Eastern Market–L'Enfant Plaza; Woodley Park–Adams Morgan–McPherson Square Metro; Congress Heights–Union Station; National Mall. Full details of the routes and operating hours can be found on the website (dccirculator.com).

TAXIS

● Taxis are abundant and safe in Washington. Look for cars with white lights on their roof tops, which signal they are for hire. Fares are $3.50 upon entering the cab and $2.16 for each additional mile. Other charges that may be added include luggage at $0.50 a piece; if you're coming from the airport, there's an additional charge of $4; each additional passenger is $1.

DRIVING

● Driving in Washington is for the patient only.
● Although "right turn on red" is permitted in most places, most Downtown intersections have signs forbidding it from 7am to 7pm, or banning it outright where there are a lot of pedestrians. Virginia also allows "left turn on red" when a vehicle is turning into a one-way street from another one-way street.
● The speed limit in the city varies from street to street; the maximum speed limit in residential areas is 25mph (40kph).
● Don't exceed the speed limits, as there are hidden cameras in popular areas.
● Seat belts are mandatory.

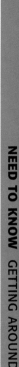

CAR RENTAL

Alamo ☎ 888/826-6893
Avis ☎ 800/633-3469
Budget ☎ 800/218-7992
Dollar ☎ 800/800-4000
Hertz ☎ 800/654-3131
National ☎ 844/382-6875
You will have to provide a credit card and those drivers under 25 years old may have to pay a local surcharge.

PARKING IN D.C.

Parking is a problem in Washington, as the public parking areas fill up quickly with local workers' cars. If you park on city streets, check the signs to make sure it is permitted: Green-and-white signs show when parking is allowed, red-and-white signs when it is not. Parking on most main streets is not permitted during rush hours, and if you park illegally your car is likely to get towed. If it does, call ☎ Dept. of Motor Vehicles 202/737-4404 to find out where it is and how to get it back. If it is towed on a weekend (after 7pm Friday) you'll have to wait until Monday to retrieve it.

Essential Facts

NEED TO KNOW ESSENTIAL FACTS

MONEY

The unit of currency is the dollar (= 100 cents). Notes (bills) come in denominations of $1, $2, $5, $10, $20, $50 and $100; coins come in 25¢ (a quarter), 10¢ (a dime), 5¢ (a nickel) and 1¢ (a penny).

TAXES

Sales tax in Washington, D.C. is 6 percent, hotel tax 14.95 percent (varies in Virginia) and food and beverage tax 10.25 percent.

BASIC NEEDS

Bed, Bath and Beyond sells voltage converters (709 7th Street NW; tel 202/628-0002; bedbathandbeyond. com). For shoe repairs, try Cobbler's Bench (40 Massachusetts Avenue NE and other locations; cobblersbenchshoe repair.com).

CUSTOMS

● Visitors aged 18 or over (21 for alcohol), may import duty free: 200 cigarettes or 100 cigars; 1 liter (1 U.S. quart) of alcohol; and gifts up to $100 in value.
● Restricted import items include meat, seeds, plants and fruit.
● Some medication bought over the counter abroad may be available by prescription-only in the U.S. and may be confiscated. For safety, bring a doctor's certificate for essential medication.

ELECTRICITY

● The electricity supply is 110 volts AC, and plugs are standard two pins. Foreign visitors will need an adaptor and may also need a voltage converter for their own appliances.

EMBASSIES AND CONSULATES

● Canada at 501 Pennsylvania Avenue NW (tel 202/682-1740, canada.ca/canada-in-washington).
● Ireland at 2234 Massachusetts Avenue NW (tel 202/462-3939, embassyofireland.org).
● UK at 3100 Massachusetts Avenue NW (tel 202/588-6500, gov.uk/world/organisations/british-embassy-washington).

EMERGENCY PHONE NUMBERS

● Police 911
● Fire 911
● Ambulance 911
● For all other non-urgent matters 311.

LOST PROPERTY

● Metro or Metrobus, tel 202/962-1195
● Smithsonian museums, tel 202/633-5630
● Other lost articles, call the city on 311.

MAIL

There are several post offices around the city.
● The National Capitol location has the longest hours at 2 Massachusetts Avenue NE (tel 202/636-1259, open Mon–Fri 9–7, Sat–Sun 9–5).

- Farragut, 1800 M Street NW, tel 202/636-1259, Mon–Fri 9–5.
- L'Enfant Plaza, 470 L'Enfant Plaza SW, tel 202/268-4970, Mon–Fri 8–5.
- Washington Square, 1050 Connecticut Avenue NW, tel 202/636-1259, Mon–Fri 9–5.
- Union Station, 50 Massachusetts Avenue NE, tel 202/636-1259, Mon–Fri 7.30–5, Sat 7.30–3.30.

MEDICAL TREATMENT

- The hospital closest to Downtown is George Washington University Hospital (900 23rd Street NW, tel 202/715-4000).
- Try Inn House Doctor for urgent care visits to Washington, D.C. hotels (tel 800/654-2504 or ask at the front desk of your hotel).
- The D.C. Dental Society operates an online referral service (dcdental.org).
- Walgreens operates a daily 24-hour pharmacy at 1217 22nd Street NW (tel 202/776-9084).

MONEY MATTERS

- Credit cards are widely accepted in hotels, restaurants and shops, but some retailers may impose a surcharge.
- Tipping is expected for all services. As a guide the following applies:
Restaurants: 15–20 percent
Bartenders: 15–20 percent per round of drinks
Hairdressers: 15–20 percent
Taxis: 15 percent
Chambermaids: $2 per day
Porters: $2 per bag.

NEWSPAPERS AND MAGAZINES

- Washington has two major daily newspapers, *The Washington Post* and *The Washington Times*, which is more conservative.
- The *Washington City Paper*, a free weekly with an emphasis on entertainment, is available from newspaper boxes around town and at many restaurants, clubs and other outlets (washingtoncitypaper.com).

STREET NAMES

Washington's street names are based on a quadrant system, the center of which is the Capitol building. Numbered streets run north–south, while lettered streets run east–west. Both progress with distance from the Capitol. There is no "J" Street, so as to prevent confusion with "I" Street. For example, 1900 R Street NW is 19 blocks west and 17 blocks north of the Capitol, as "R" is the 17th letter if you skip "J." Diagonal avenues cut across the grid. They are named after the States based on their date of statehood and their proximity to the Capitol. Delaware, the "First State," is closest.

RADIO

- FM Radio 88.5 (WAMU)—public radio (news)
- 90.9 (WETA)—classical
- 98.7 (WMZQ)—country
- 99.5 (WIHT)—pop
- 101.1 (WWD.C.)—rock

LOCAL BLOGS

- dc.eater.com/—the place for foodies, area restaurant news and reviews.
- dcist.com—thorough news and goings-on site.
- washingtonpost.com/goingoutguide—postings by *The Washington Post*'s team of experts.

- In addition, various neighborhood weekly newspapers serve Capitol Hill, Adams Morgan and other areas.
- *Washingtonian*, a monthly magazine, has a calendar of events, dining information, arts reviews and articles about the city and its prominent people.
- *Where/Washington*, a monthly magazine listing popular things to do, is free at most hotels.
- Other national newspapers are available.

OPENING HOURS

- Stores generally open Mon–Sat 10–6, Sun 12–5 with shopping malls open longer.
- Banks open Mon–Fri 9–5, although hours can vary, with a handful open on weekends.
- Post offices open Mon–Fri 9–5, with some offices open Sat.

PUBLIC HOLIDAYS

- Jan 1: New Year's Day
- Third Mon in Jan: Birthday of Martin Luther King, Jr.
- Third Mon in Feb: Presidents' Day
- Last Mon in May: Memorial Day
- Jul 4: Independence Day
- First Mon in Sep: Labor Day
- Second Mon in Oct: Columbus Day
- Nov 11: Veterans Day
- Fourth Thu in Nov: Thanksgiving Day
- Dec 25: Christmas Day
- On public holidays, banks and post offices close while many stores and restaurants stay open.

SMOKING

- D.C. is becoming less and less friendly to those who want to light up. Smoking is banned in almost all indoor public places, including restaurants, bars and clubs.

STATE REGULATIONS

- You must be 21 years old to drink alcohol in Washington, and you may be required to produce proof of age and photo ID.

STUDENTS

● Holders of an International Student Identity Card may be entitled to discounts at some clothing and electronic stores, theaters, cinemas and restaurants.

VISITOR INFORMATION

● Destination D.C. is at 901 7th Street NW, 4th Floor, Washington, D.C., 20001 (tel 202/789-7000, washington.org).

● National Park Service is at 1849 C Street NW, Washington, D.C., 20240 (tel 202/208-6843, nps.gov).

● Comprehensive information about D.C.'s many public transportation options and how they connect visitors to locals events is at goDCgo.com (202/299-2186).

● The White House Visitor Center is located at Baldrige Hall in the Department of Commerce Building, 1450 Pennsylvania Avenue NW (tel 202/208-1631; nps.gov/whho, open daily 7.30–4).

● For recorded information on exhibits and special offerings at Smithsonian Institution museums, tel 202/633-1000.

● Discounted tickets for the theater, concerts, ballet, opera, cinema and galleries can be found at TodayTix (todaytix.com).

WASHINGTON SLANG

● "Hill staffers"—staff for individual members of Congress who work on Capitol Hill. Dominant demographic in D.C.

● "Inside the Beltway"—the Beltway (I-495) forms a circle around the District. This refers to the American political system and its insularity.

● "Foggy Bottom," "Langley"—agencies are often referred to by their location. These are the State Department and CIA, respectively.

● "NoVa"—short for "Northern Virginia," this typically refers to Arlington and Alexandria. Occasionally used as a term of derision.

● "DelMarVa"—describes the three-state Mid-Atlantic region consisting of Delaware, Maryland and Virginia.

TELEPHONES

● To call Washington from the UK, dial 00 1, Washington's area code (202), and then the number.

● To call the UK from Washington, dial 011 44, then omit the first zero from the area code.

SAFETY

Washington is as safe as any large city, but the usual commonsense rules apply. Because of the wide income divide, crime statistics vary hugely from block to block. Tourist areas that are safe during the day may not be safe at night. At night, walk with someone rather than alone; use taxis in less populous areas.

NEED TO KNOW ESSENTIAL FACTS

Timeline

EARLY DAYS

In 1779, President George Washington was authorized by Congress to build a Federal City. The following year, he hired Pierre Charles L'Enfant to design a city beside the Potomac River. According to legend, he sited the U.S. Capitol in the exact middle of the 13 original states. By 1800, President Adams was able to occupy the unfinished White House, and Congress met in the Capitol, also unfinished. The population was by then around 3,000.

DOWN THE WIRE

In 1844, Samuel F. B. Morse transmitted the first telegraph message from the Capitol to Baltimore, Maryland.

1812 The U.S. declares war on Britain in response to the impressment of sailors from American ships and border disputes in Canada.

1814 The British sack Washington, burning the White House and the Capitol. The war ends with the Treaty of Ghent, ratified in late 1814.

1846 Congress accepts James Smithson's bequest and establishes the Smithsonian Institution.

1850 The slave trade is abolished in the District of Columbia.

1863 President Abraham Lincoln's Emancipation Proclamation frees the nation's slaves; many move to Washington.

1865 Lincoln is assassinated during a performance at Ford's Theatre.

1867 Howard University is chartered by Congress to educate black people.

1876 The nation's centennial is celebrated with a fair in Philadelphia.

1901 The McMillan Commission oversees the city's beautification.

1907 Trains run to the new Union Station.

1922 The Lincoln Memorial is completed, 57 years after Lincoln's death.

1943 The Jefferson Memorial and Pentagon are completed.

1974 The Watergate building becomes infamous as the site of the bungled Republican robbery attempt on Democrat headquarters. President Nixon resigns as a result of the ensuing cover-up.

1981 President Ronald Reagan is shot outside the Washington Hilton.

1991 Mayor Sharon Pratt is the first African-American woman to lead a major U.S. city.

2001 Terrorists hijack a passenger plane from Dulles Airport on September 11 and crash it into the Pentagon, killing many people.

2009 Barack Obama, the first African-American president, is inaugurated.

2011 The Martin Luther King, Jr. Memorial is dedicated to the civil rights leader.

2015 District Councilwoman Muriel Bowser is sworn in as the seventh mayor of D.C.

2017 Half a million people participate in the Women's March on Washington, the largest single-day political protest in U.S. history.

2020 This year is the 100th anniversary of the passage of the 19th Amendment, guaranteeing women's constitutional right to vote in the U.S.

"I HAVE A DREAM"

On August 28, 1963, Martin Luther King, Jr. delivered his vision of racial harmony from the steps of the Lincoln Memorial to a crowd of 200,000. Born in 1929, King had entered the ministry in 1955. As pastor of the Dexter Avenue Baptist Church in Montgomery, Alabama, he became the figurehead of the organized nonviolent civil rights protests to end discrimination laws. His "I Have a Dream" speech ended a march on Washington by blacks and whites calling for reform. King was awarded the Nobel Peace Prize in 1964. His last sermon was at Washington National Cathedral in 1968—he was shot five days later in Memphis.

Below from far left to right: Martin Luther King, Jr.; Smithsonian Institute; Union Station; Vietnam Women's Memorial; George Washington

NEED TO KNOW TIMELINE

Index

A

accommodation 107–112
  bed-and-breakfast 109
  booking agency 112
  hotels 108, 109–112
Adams Morgan 7, 10, 13
African-American Civil War
  Memorial and Museum 88
airports 116–117
  airlines 117
Anacostia Community Museum
  102
Anderson House 88, 89
Arlington National Cemetery
  8, 98–99
art and antiques 12, 77, 90,
  91, 104

B

basketball 67
bike hire 78, 118
Bishop's Garden 18, 88
booking agency 112
bookstores 10, 12, 66, 77,
  90, 91
Botanic Gardens see
  U.S. Botanic Garden
budget travelers 17, 109
Bureau of Engraving and
  Printing 49
buses 118, 119
  long-distance 116

C

cafés 15, 31, 52, 68, 80, 93
Capitol Building see
  U.S. Capitol Building
Capitol Hill 4, 53–68
  entertainment and nightlife
    13, 67
  map 54–55
  shopping 66
  sights 57–64
  walk 65
  where to eat 68
car rental 119
children
  children's shops 12, 66
  entertainment 18
cinema 13, 67
Clara Barton Missing Soldiers
  Office Museum 26
classical music venues 67,
  74, 105
climate and seasons 114
clubs and bars 13, 17
  see also entertainment
    and nightlife
customs regulations 120

D

DAR Museum 26
D.C. Circulator 119

disabilities, visitors with 118
Discovery Theater 18, 49
Douglass, Frederick 100
Downtown 20–32
  entertainment and nightlife 30
  map 22–23
  shopping 29
  sights 24–27
  walk 28
  where to eat 31–32
driving 119
Dumbarton Oaks 18, 75
Dupont Circle 7, 13, 88, 89

E

Eastern Market 65, 66
eating out 14, 15, 18
  see also where to eat
electricity 120
embassies and consulates 120
emergency phone numbers 120
entertainment and nightlife 13
  Capitol Hill 67
  Downtown 30
  Farther Afield 105
  Georgetown/Foggy Bottom
    78–79
  Northwest Washington 92
excursions 103

F

Farther Afield 95–106
  entertainment and nightlife
    105
  excursions 103
  map 96–97
  shopping 104
  sights 98–102
  where to eat 106
fashion shopping 10, 12, 16, 29,
  73, 77, 90, 91, 104
FDR Memorial 7, 8, 36, 51
festivals and events 114
Folger Shakespeare Library and
  Theatre 64, 67
food and drink
  alcohol regulations 122
  coffee culture 31
  shopping for 11, 12, 66, 90
  see also where to eat
Ford's Theatre 28, 30
Frederick Douglass National
  Historic Site 8, 100–101
Fredericksburg 103
Freer|Sackler:
  The Smithsonian's Museums
  of Asian Art 11, 49

G

Georgetown/Foggy Bottom
  69–80
  entertainment and nightlife
    78–79

  map 70–71
  shopping 9, 73, 77–78
  sights 73–75
  walk 76
  where to eat 80
George Washington's Mount
  Vernon 4, 11, 103
George Washington University
  Museum—The Textile
  Museum 75
Grant Memorial 64, 65

H

half-price tickets 78
Hirshhorn Museum and
  Sculpture Garden 49
history 4, 5, 124–125
hotels 16, 108, 109–112

I

insurance 117
International Spy Museum
  9, 37
Islamic Center 88

J

Japanese American Memorial
  to Patriotism During World
  War II 64
Jefferson Memorial 7, 8, 36,
  51
Jefferson, Thomas 24, 36, 57
John F. Kennedy Center 7, 9, 16,
  17, 74, 76

K

Kennedy, John F. 74, 87, 98, 99
King, Jr., Martin Luther 7, 38,
  39, 51, 125
Korean War Veterans
  Memorial 49, 51
Kreeger Museum 75

L

L'Enfant, Pierre Charles 4, 28,
  51, 99, 124
Library of Congress 9, 10,
  56–57, 65
Lincoln, Abraham 28, 38, 51,
  57, 60, 124
Lincoln Memorial 7, 9, 28, 38,
  39, 51, 124
lost property 120

M

Madame Tussauds 26
mail 120–121
The Mall 4, 33–52
  map 34–35
  shopping 52
  sights 36–50
  walk 51
  where to eat 52

malls 10, 12, 29, 66, 104
markets 66, 68
Martin Luther King, Jr.
    Memorial 7, 9, 39
medical and dental treatment
    121
medication (regulations for
    travel) 120
Metro 4, 118–119
money 120, 121

N
National Air and Space
    Museum 9, 11, 40, 52, 67
National Arboretum 18, 102
National Archives 9, 28, 41
National Building Museum
    11, 18, 26
National Gallery of Art 6, 9, 11,
    17, 28, 42, 51, 52
National Gallery of Art
    Sculpture Garden 49–50
National Geographic Museum
    26
National Museum of African
    American History and
    Culture (NMAAHC) 9, 11,
    43
National Museum of African
    Art 11
National Museum of American
    History 11, 18, 50
National Museum of the
    American Indian 6, 9, 11,
    44, 52
National Museum of Natural
    History 11, 18, 28,
    50, 52
National Museum of Women
    in the Arts 27
National Portrait Gallery 27,
    28
National Postal Museum 64
National World War II
    Memorial 50, 51
National Zoological Park 7,
    9, 17, 84
newspapers and magazines
    121–122
Northwest Washington
    81–94
    entertainment and nightlife
        92
    map 82–83
    shopping 90–91
    sights 84–88
    walk 89
    where to eat 93–94

O
Old Stone House 75
Old Town, Alexandria 102
opening hours 122

P
parking 119
passports and visas 116, 117
Pentagon 4, 125
Phillips Collection 9, 85, 89
political ephemera 11
post offices 120–121, 122
Potomac River 76
public holidays 122
public transportation 115,
    118–119

R
radio 122
Reflecting Pool 38, 51
Renwick Gallery 27
Rock Creek Park 8, 17, 86

S
safety, personal 123
Shakespeare Theatre 6, 17, 30
shopping 10–12, 16, 18
    Capitol Hill 66
    Downtown 29
    Farther Afield 104
    Georgetown/Foggy Bottom
        73, 77–78
    The Mall 52
    museum shops 11, 52
    Northwest Washington 90–91
    opening hours 122
Shrine of the Immaculate
    Conception 102
slang terms 123
Smithsonian American Art
    Museum (SAAM) 11, 27
smoking 122
souvenirs 11
spas 17, 104
speeding 119
sports 67
state regulations 122
Steven F. Udvar-Hazy Center
    40
street names 121
student travelers 123
Studio Gallery 88

T
taxes 120
taxis 119
telephones 123
temperatures 114
theater 17, 18, 30, 49, 67, 74,
    92, 105
Theodore Roosevelt Island
    102
ticket outlets 78
Tidal Basin 36, 47, 51
time differences 114
tipping 121
Top 25 sights 8–9
train services 116

U
U Street 88
Union Market 68
Union Station 6, 66
U.S. Botanic Garden 8, 28,
    58–59, 65
U.S. Capitol 4, 5, 6, 8, 11, 28,
    51, 60–61, 65
U.S. Holocaust Memorial
    Museum 8, 45
U.S. Supreme Court Building
    8, 62–63

V
Vietnam Veterans Memorial
    8, 48, 51
views over the city 6, 7, 16,
    30, 46, 47, 51, 65, 74, 76,
    100, 103
visitor information 115, 123

W
walks
    Capitol Hill 65
    Downtown 28
    Georgetown/Foggy
        Bottom 76
    The Mall 51
    Northwest Washington 89
Washington, George 103,
    108, 124
Washington Monument 6, 7, 8,
    16, 28, 46–47, 51, 65
Washington National
    Cathedral 8, 18, 87
Watergate building 76, 125
websites 115, 122
What's On 114
Where to Eat 14, 15, 16, 18
    Capitol Hill 68
    Downtown 31–32
    Farther Afield 106
    Georgetown/Foggy
        Bottom 80
    The Mall 52
    Northwest Washington 93–94
White House, The 5, 6, 8,
    24–25, 28, 124
Woodrow Wilson House
    Museum 88
World Bank Group Visitor
    Center 27

Z
zoo 7, 9, 17, 84

Washington, D.C. 25 Best

WRITTEN BY Mary Case, Bruce Walker and Matthew Cordell
UPDATED BY Anita Sach and David Leck
SERIES EDITOR Clare Ashton
COVER DESIGN Jessica Gonzalez
DESIGN WORK Liz Baldin
IMAGE RETOUCING AND REPRO Ian Little

ISBN 978-1-64097-328-2

FOURTEENTH EDITION

All details in this book are based on information supplied to us at press time. Always confirm information when it matters, especially if you're making a detour to visit a specific place. Fodor's expressly disclaims any liability, loss, or risk, personal or otherwise, that is incurred as a consequence of the use of any of the contents of this book.

Printed and bound in China by 1010 Printing Group Limited.

10 9 8 7 6 5 4 3 2 1

A05743
Maps in this title produced from mapping © MAIRDUMONT / Falk Verlag 2013 and data available from openstreetmap.org © under the Open Database License found at opendatacommons.org
Transport map © Communicarta Ltd, UK

We would like to thank the following photographers, companies and picture libraries for their assistance in the preparation of this book:

2, 3, 4t, 4l, 5t AA/C Sawyer; 5c Courtesy of Washington.org; 6t, 6cl, 6c, 6cr, 6bl, 6bc AA/C Sawyer; 6br AA/E Davies; 7t, 7tl AA/C Sawyer; 7tc AA/E Davies; 7tr AA/C Sawyer; 7bl AA/E Davies; 7bc AA/E Davies; 7br, 8t, 9t, 10t, 10tr AA/C Sawyer; 10ct Courtesy of Washington.org; 10cb AA/C Sawyer; 10b Courtesy of Washington.org; 11t, 11l AA/C Sawyer; 11ct AA/M Jourdan; 11cb AA/H Harris; 11b Courtesy of Washington.org; 12t, 13t AA/C Sawyer; 13tl Brand X Pics; 13ct Courtesy of Washington.org; 13c, 13cb Digital Vision; 13b RosalreneBetancourt1/ Alamy; 14t, 14tr AA/C Sawyer; 14ct AA/J Love; 14cb ImageState; 14b AA/J Love; 15t AA/C Sawyer; 16tr AA/J Love; 16t AA/C Sawyer; 16cr AA/J Love; 16/7b AA/J Love; 17t AA/C Sawyer; 17tl, 17tl, 18t AA/J Love; 18cr Courtesy of Washington.org; 18br Mark Summerfield/Alamy Stock Photo; 20/1 AA/C Sawyer; 24/5 Courtesy of Washington.org; 25tr, 25cr Michael Ventura/Alamy Stock Photo; 26t Courtesy of Washington.org; 26b K. L. Howard/Alamy; 27t Courtesy of Washington.org; 27b National Portrait Gallery/Smithsonian; 28 AA/C Sawyer; 29tAA/H Harris; 30 PhotoDisc; 31, 32 Greg Powers/Jaleo; 33 AA/C Sawyer; 36l Blaine Harrington III/ Alamy; 36r AA/E Davies; 37l Richard T. Nowitz/CORBIS; 37r Spy Museum; 38l, 38c, 38r AA/C Sawyer; 39l joeysworld.com/Alamy; 39r RGB Ventures LLC dba SuperStock/Alamy; 40l AA/J Love; 40r David R. Frazier Photolibrary, Inc./Alamy; 41l K. L. Howard/Alamy; 41r AA/E Davies; 42l David Coleman/Alamy; 42r, 43l Courtesy of Washington.org; 43r Courtesy of the NMAAHC/Smithsonian Institution; 44l, 44c, 44r, 45l, 45c, 45r AA/J Love; 46l, 46/7tc, 46/47bc AA/C Sawyer; 47l AA/E Davies; 47r, 48l, 48r AA/C Sawyer; 49t NPS Photo; 49b AA/C Sawyer; 50t NPS Photo; 50bl National Museum of American History; 50br Courtesy of Washington.org; 51 AA/C Sawyer; 52t Digital Vision; 52c AA/D Corrance; 53, 56 AA/C Sawyer; 57l AA/E Davies; 57r Library of Congress/Shawn Miller; 58 U.S. Botanic Garden; 59tl AA/E Davies; 59tr, 59c U.S. Botanic Garden; 60l, 60/1tc AA/C Sawyer; 60/61bc Courtesy of Washington.org; 61l, 61r AA/C Sawyer; 62 AA/J Love; 63l, 63r AA/C Sawyer; 64t Courtesy of Washington.org; 64b Andre Jenny/Alamy; 65, 66 AA/C Sawyer; 67 PhotoDisc; 68 AA/P Bennett; 69 AA/J Love; 72 Sean Pavone/Alamy Stock Photo; 73l, 73r Courtesy of Washington.org; 74l, 74r AA/C Sawyer; 75t Dumbarton Oaks; 75bl William Atkins/The George Washington University; 75br Dumbarton Oaks; 76 AA/C Sawyer; 77t, 78t Andriy Blokhin/Alamy Stock Photo; 78c, 79t Digital Vision; 80 AA/C Sawyer; 81 Courtesy of Washington.org; 84 Smithsonian's National Zoo; 85 Courtesy of Phillips Collection; 86l, 86r courtesy of Rock Creek Park; 87l, 87r AA/J Love; 88t Courtesy of Washington.org; 89, 90, 91 AA/C Sawyer; 92 Brand X Pics; 93 AA/P Bennett; 94 AA/P Bennett; 95 AA/J Love; 98, 98/9t AA/C Sawyer; 98/9c, 99r, 100l AA/E Davies; 100r AA/C Sawyer; 101 AA/J Love; 102t Courtesy of Washington.org; 102bl AA/N Ray; 102br AA/J Love; 103t, 103bl, 103br AA/E Davies; 104 AA/S McBride; 105 Digital Vision; 106 AA/C Sawyer; 108t AA/C Sawyer; 108tr PhotoDisc; 108ct AA/C Sawyer; 108cb, 108b PhotoDisc; 109, 110, 111, 112 AA/C Sawyer; 114, 115, 116, 117, 118t AA/C Sawyer; 118b AA/E Davies; 119t, 120, 121, 122t, 123, 124t AA/C Sawyer; 124bl Hulton Archive/Getty Images; 124bc AA/C Sawyer; 124/5b AA/E Davies; 125t, 125bc AA/C Sawyer; 125br AA/AA.

Every effort has been made to trace the copyright holders, and we apologise in advance for any unintentional omissions or errors. We would be pleased to apply any corrections in a following edition of this publication.

Titles in the Series

- Amsterdam
- Bangkok
- Barcelona
- Berlin
- Boston
- Brussels and Bruges
- Budapest
- Chicago
- Dubai
- Dublin
- Edinburgh
- Florence
- Hong Kong
- Istanbul
- Krakow
- Las Vegas
- Lisbon
- London
- Madrid
- Melbourne
- Milan
- Montréal
- Munich
- New York City
- Orlando
- Paris
- Rome
- San Francisco
- Seattle
- Shanghai
- Singapore
- Sydney
- Tokyo
- Toronto
- Venice
- Vienna
- Washington, D.C.